GW00501808

CYPRUS
Things The Estate Agents
Don't Tell You

by

Pete Thenshorn

Grosvenor House
Publishing Limited

All rights reserved
Copyright © Pete Thenshorn, 2006
www.ThingsTheEstateAgentsDontTellYou.com

Pete Thenshorn is hereby identified as author of this
work in accordance with Section 77 of the Copyright, Designs
and Patents Act 1988

The book cover picture is copyright to Zen Zebra
www.caricaturecan.com

This book is published by
Grosvenor House Publishing Ltd
28-30 High Street, Guildford, Surrey, GU1 3HY.
www.grosvenorhousepublishing.co.uk

Whilst this book is based on personal experiences, all names of
characters, companies and Estate Agents are a product of
the author's imagination. So any resemblances in names
to any person or company are entirely coincidental.

This book is sold subject to the conditions that it shall not, by way of
trade or otherwise, be lent, resold, hired out or otherwise circulated
without the author's or publisher's prior consent in any form of binding or
cover other than that in which it is published and
without a similar condition including this condition being imposed
on the subsequent purchaser.

A CIP record for this book
is available from the British Library

ISBN 1-905529-70-8

Dedication

To Lara's parents, thanks for all their help and much needed support. Without them this could have been a much different story.

Thanks to my parents for being there.

Most of all, thanks to Lara, my proof reader, my encouragement, my partner in crime and my everything. Without her to share the ups and the downs a nervous breakdown would have surely ensued.

And lest I forget, thanks to Del, his son, and their team of illegal immigrant workers for all their hard work. You know who you really are!!!☺

Introduction

I'd like to start by saying that Cyprus is a truly wonderful country. Its beauty for me is not just in the fact that the sun shines
and the sky's blue for most of the year or that it has some fantastic beaches. For me, Cyprus's real wonder is in it's variety; from
the serenity and magnificence of the Troodos mountains to the
hidden coves of Kapparis to name but a few, and all of which are
within one hours drive from each other. It takes less time to go
from swimming in the sea to hiking in the pine filled mountains
than it does to travel from one smog filled congested side of
London to the other.

But this book is not a book to promote the beauties of
Cyprus as many as there undoubtedly are! I'm sure there are
already quite enough of those. It's not meant to be your bog
standard tourist guide or glossy developers bumph designed
with one purpose in mind.....to sell! Be it a holiday or a villa.
No, this book is not and was not written to be any of the above.
This book was written with one purpose in mind and that was
quite simply to tell the truth. No bullshit. Something that most
of the former sadly could never boast since it is the very fact that
they are trying to sell you something that stops them from ever
being able to really do so. After all, nobody in their right minds
would tell you the bad things about their product, would they?

Sometimes in life it gets to the point where you feel
compelled to tell it as it really is- to cut away the fat and sift
through the shit that obstructs our view- to find that illusive but
very real place called "The Truth!" And when you've finally

discovered it, to guide others less fortunate than yourself to it. However, sometimes to guide them can in itself be the most difficult thing. Some people just don't want to see the truth. They actually want to believe the hype. They long to live the dream, to walk the walk as I suppose did we. But I'm here to try to drag them, kicking and screaming if necessary, to it. That's why I'm quite simply going to tell you our story and then give to you the facts that we have learnt about buying, selling and renting property in Cyprus. In doing so, we hope that you can be enlightened a little and at least stand a chance against the bullshit that is readily dished out to the unsuspecting tourist looking to invest some of his or hers hard earned cash. I'm not saying that these are all the pitfalls and interesting points to property in Cyprus by any means, just the ones that we have stumbled across mostly through hard experience and great expense. So my advice to you is to read carefully and make notes. But most of all beware of the ones that we don't know about, as I'm sure there are still quite a few pitfalls left for even us to fall down in this land of sun, sea and sand that we lovingly call Cyprus!!!

Whilst I have tried to be very honest in this book, I must add that this book is only based on our personal experience out here over the past year. Maybe they'll be others out there who have had completely different experiences. Who knows? It's specifically about our experiences in property and with Estate Agents and others like them. All names have of course been changed to protect the innocent, namely us!!! I am not the world's best writer just an every day bod like you who's just trying to tell it as it is, maybe with a sprinkling of salt and pepper here and there to add a little flavour ☺. We simply hope that in reading this you might learn from our mistakes and thus bypass some of the stress that we've incurred in the past couple of years here in sunny Cyprus.

CHAPTER 1

Our Story

My name is Pete and my lovely wife is called Lara. Our story is one of two relatively young thirty something's who gave up their day jobs, well paid as they were, to go in search of that "Place in the sun/Grand design/Property ladder dream" that has been cleverly spoon-fed into the homes of every TV owning Brit for the past few years. Like a drug we've craved more and more of these sticky tape shows. More and more of the fantasy. A fantasy that's made us ever discontent with our semi-detached houses, our gardens, our country and our very lives. A drug that has slowly corroded away our natural defence systems and left us easy prey to the most ferocious of animals in today's society. The animals we like to refer to as "Estate Agents!"

It was eleven o'clock on a sunny May morning 2005 and our shipping container had started to be loaded. We had sold our lovely house of 6 years and replaced it for one big, red, rusty old metal container which stank of salty damp. It was being stuffed to the brim with all of our worldly possessions- beds, sofas, pots, pans, coffee table, cuddly toys etc. Our entire life's worth all in one container. Destination- Cyprus. Land of sun, sea, Turkish delights, oops sorry I meant to say Cyprus delights and of course "the lowest crime rate in Europe". At least that's what it says in all the brochures. If it is the lowest then it's probably because the courts system is so slow that no one can ever be bothered to actually report the crimes. Anyway, Cyprus was our destination good or bad!!!

It all really began about a year ago, 2004… We like many other young couples at the time found ourselves with extra cash. We were one of the fortunate ones who had benefited from the rise in the British property market and found ourselves with both huge equity in our house and substantial savings in the bank. Yeah, we had lost a little in shares like every other bod who had ridden the IT bubble and got caught on the top when it burst, but over all we were in a fantastic financial situation. Not millionaires but not paupers either! Our dilemma was that we had all this surplus cash and wanted to invest it into something else. The problem now was that the property market in Britain was hugely overpriced. So the old buy-to-let thing didn't seem such a good proposition anymore since you were paying way too much for the property in the first place. You really needed to get in on that one a few years earlier when prices were lower and the returns were higher. And, as I just said we had just had our fingers burnt with shares so we didn't fancy going there again. It was a dilemma, a good dilemma but a dilemma never the less!!!

I was interested in buying up North, as property prices were lower up there but a friend of ours suggested speaking to a financial adviser he knew. Not a bad idea we thought so we booked an appointment with him. A huge monster of a cigar smoking Cypriot called Ben. Much to Lara's upset, Ben barely acknowledged her presence. Looking back I think he was just trying to give us a taster of things to come! Ben hardly listened to our ideas of purchasing property up North. He was dead set against this idea and instead gave us his long schpeil on how his customers have been asking the very same question, "Where should they invest"? He explained to us how, because of this reoccurring question, he has conducted an extensive survey into it. The conclusion he had come to after his so called extensive survey was that... surprise, surprise... Cyprus was the best place to invest at this moment in time. He told us how it had been achieving a year on year growth in property prices of twenty percent and how this was projected to continue for the next few years. It was as he pulled out from under his desk a wadge of crisp brochures for Arbo Developers' new build projects, that Lara and I looked at each other and had the exact same thought.

This financial adviser had just morphed right in front of our eyes. He had morphed into the very thing we both hated the most. An Estate Agent. With one very clear objective to sell, sell, sell. Arbo was obviously his master and according to him Arbo properties were the only ones developing good quality projects and Paphos was the place to buy. Of course it just so happened that Paphos was the exact area where these new builds that he had to offer us were. What a stroke of luck eh? Cyprus was certainly an idea, but we weren't so sure about buying off plan. When I dared to ask about resales in Cyprus he rapidly dismissed the idea with a firm hand and insisted on these new builds. I suspected there was not as much commission in resales for him. The truth is, commission and backhanders is what really makes the economy turn in Cyprus. Everybody's taking some sort of cut. So don't believe anything they tell you as they've got only one thing on their minds and it sure as hell ain't your health. Needless to say when our meeting was over we were pretty relieved to get out of there. But our meeting with Ben had planted the idea in our heads that maybe investing in another country was a definite option and something to look into.

When we got back home we did some research ourselves, and sure enough Cyprus was getting rave reviews and what you could get for your cash was outstanding compared to England. It also had a lot of plus points over other European countries.

For instance, Spain was really now quite overpriced. The advantage it had over the other in places such as Bulgaria and Romania was that it had virtually the same system of law as England. This was because it had been a British colony for many years. In short this meant that purchasing was relatively easy and safe. It had also just become a member of the EU so we, as EU citizens, could purchase with the usual protective structures that being a member of the EU encompasses. Because of its newly acquired EU statues people were keen to invest hence prices were continuing to rocket. All these things certainly made it an appealing prospect. However, I was still interested in investing up North. I wasn't completely sold on the idea of Cyprus. It really took a couple of what I then considered to be coincidences to make our minds up. One of these coincidences was that, about a day later I found out that my mate and his family had purchased in Cyprus. It turned out that his brother, who I also knew, had just moved out there. The last but most convincing coincidence was that later the same evening there was a whole half an hour TV documentary saying how fantastic Cyprus was. Well that was it for us. We were sold. All it took was a TV show…. typical!!!

Without delay we made arrangements and booked two tickets to Cyprus on good old Cyprus Airways. Within two weeks of the TV show we landed in Cyprus with only one objective, to buy, buy, buy… like lambs to the slaughter!

We had booked a one week stay in Wondering Kings Apartments, Paphos. Well that was a joke for a start, because there was no king alive except perhaps for the king of wishful thinking who would not have been seen dead in these scraggly old apartments. However, it didn't matter as I had picked up the keys to my mate's apartment in Limassol to use if things got too bad. This was to be no holiday however. We looked at this trip as business and intended to treat it as so. Our intension was to get up at eight every morning, hire a car and get to as many Estate Agents as humanly possible.

When we arrived in Paphos we couldn't believe how much building was actually going on. So much for Arbo being the only developer, there were hundreds of them squeezing developments into every conceivable crevice. It's a standing joke now for us, we call Cyprus the building site of the world. At the moment it really is one big building site. Like all foolish tourists we hired a convertible Vitara. If you're planning to go over and hire a car, my advice to you is do not go for a convertible Vitara. As we soon found out, as romantic as a convertible sounds, in the scorching heat of the Cyprus sun the last thing you want is the roof down. In that sort of heat you would give your kingdom for a decent roof to shade you from the sun. Anyway in our defence it was the only car they had, so we didn't really have much choice.

Once we picked up the car we were off! No "sigar sigar" for us. Our plan was to look for a resale apartment. Something with a sea view that probably needed a bit of work. We weren't so sold on off plans as you hear all sorts of stories of people never getting their buildings built! So we figured that at least with a resale you could see what you were getting.

We hit all the agents with military precision. We named it operation "Cyprus Storm" but we under estimated the agent's resolve to sell us new builds. It was like a huge conspiracy to not allow any tourist the opportunity to buy resales. It was the same over and over again. We'd go into the Estate Agent and ask to see what resales they had on their books but every time after a feeble attempt at finding resales they would say the same thing. Why don't you consider purchasing off plan? It just so happens we have some fantastic developments. The ideal investment for the foreign investor such as yourselves. Blah blah blah blah blah!!!

Quite frankly it was a slaughter. We even viewed quite a few of these projects, most of which were just flattened land in the middle of nowhere usually with a donkey or two still wandering around on it. The story was always the same, "Oh and of course as you can see it's just farm land around this plot so you can be assured no other building work will happen here in the future. Your views can never be obstructed." Yeah right. Not that old chestnut. This is Cyprus after all, the building site of the world. Unless the sea is right outside your window there is always a chance of someone building a new development right smack in front of yours. Especially if it's farm land. After all, there's not as much money in farming as there used to be is there? A few backhanders here and fronthanders there and hey presto that glorious farm land has just been turned into yet another building site together with all the noise and pollution that go with it.

They would also all tell you how great the quality of build is on their fabulous projects. How their developments are the only developments with such high quality of build. Well, in our experience quality of build is not something that most of them know anything about nor care about. Quality of profit, or to be precise their five percent commission is all they are thinking about when they are reeling out the schpeil to you.

One night in Paphos Wondering Kings Apartments was enough for us. The next day we decided to head over to my mates apartment and check out Limassol. It was there in Limassol where we were introduced to Fuller Real Estates and Jed. A name that was to become a thorn in our side.

CHAPTER 2

Off Plan

It was right at the end of our first day in Limassol when we chanced across the offices of Fuller. We had been randomly popping into every Estate Agent's office that we could find since eight in the morning to see what they had on their books. By the time we came across Fuller we were completely knackered and very nearly didn't go in. Unfortunately we entered anyway. It was there inside that we met Jed! Fuller's lovable Estate Agent, if there is such a thing, and he told us all about their "unique investment opportunities" for the Fuller 22 projects up in Paphos.

Tired, we listened. These were again off plan apartments but with a twist. The idea was as follows and as Jed went on to sell us. The investors, i.e. us, would initially put in 30% of the asking price. This 30% gave the developers the finance to start the build. I quote now "Due to their size, Fuller can negotiate "wholesale" prices with medium sized, quality developers for properties in areas that are much in demand. These prices are usually around 20% below market prices."

Not bad hey!!! The twist was this. At 75% build time the initial investors, i.e. us, have two options: 1) to pay a further 60% or 2) sell them on at the new increased market value. As Jed went on to emphasise, the real idea was that you should sell at this stage at a new increased price. Increased due to the natural appreciation that was accruing year on year, plus remembering we got them at 20% below market value to being with. To be specific, according to Jed it had been rising 20% every year. The builds were deliberately slow, approximately two years from start to finish. This was so that investors could maximise on the increased market value at the 75% build stage. Obviously the whole strategy really revolved around investors selling at 75%.

Jed assured us that there would be no problem selling these properties in the current market and that Fuller would actively remarket them. Also because of the whole idea that you're never really ever going to keep these apartments it didn't really matter whether you had the best sea views or the crappy view of the car park at the back. The idea was to sell at 75% and make a whole load of profit. Everybody's happy! You've made huge amounts of profit and again I quote "returns on investment of more than 50% within a time frame of 12–18 months," and Fuller stands to make twice its 5% commission- once from the developers, when you buy off plan, and once from you when you sell at 75% build stage. He told us tall tales of others like ourselves who had purchased an apartment or two not more than a year and a half ago who had made huge profits and were so impressed that they were now investing in not one, not two but entire blocks. It all sounded unbelievably amazing. The way Jed cleverly phrased it, this was a license to print money, a no brainier, a win win situation.

Just a few things to beware of here that Jed conveniently left out. It all sounds fantastic but as we all know when we're not being blinded by the bullshit nothing's ever that easy! As it turns out, Fuller's promises of a strong marketing campaign when it comes to reselling the apartments were a load of hot air. Oh how beautiful hindsight is! Unfortunately for us we didn't have the luxury of hindsight and signed up for two. More about those later, however, I can say that living out here and talking to ex-

and current employees of the company it has become clear that there is no real active campaign for marketing these resales nor has there ever been.

Possibly this is because they realise the reality; it is always far more difficult to get investors to buy in at the 75% build stage than it is to get them to invest at the start. This is quite simply because it is far easier to extract small amounts out of people than the far larger amounts required from them to come in at the 75% stage- just a thought! This in turn leads to the question of whether you should be pickier about the ones you *do* buy if you are mad enough to buy any at all after reading any of this. The answer quite simply is "yes". Despite what Jed and others like him would have you believe, under these circumstances obviously the ones with the most desirable views etc. will of course stand the better chance of selling than the ones at the back overlooking the car parks! And, as with any market place, prices can go down as well as up! An obvious one I know but in the Estate Agents world they can only ever go one way, and that's up. Yes it appears that Fuller was once again only interested in sales and their commission, not us!

Incase you are wondering, we did ask Jed how many of these fantastic projects he had invested into. We were somewhat surprised to hear that unfortunately Fuller has a terrible company policy whereby its employees only allowed to invest in 1 off plan. We both thought that seemed terrible and felt sympathetic towards Jed only being able to invest in one property on such a good deal. Out of curiosity, I asked Jed which project he had invested into and we were both dubious over his reply… "None!" Hmm….

CHAPTER 3

Resales

We still hadn't managed to find the resale property we were after. We were looking for a one or two bedroom apartment with sea views (no surprise there), that had the potential for long term rentals. At this stage the idea of moving out permanently hadn't even crossed our minds. We liked the idea of Limassol due to its central location to the South of the island. This means that from Limassol you can get to pretty much any part of the island in an hour if you really sped or an hour and a half if you drive to the limits. Also, its economy doesn't just depend on tourism. It had the main port, so loads of off shore companies are based there. In turn this meant loads of jobs, and as a knock on effect, an ideal place for long term rentals. In Limassol there are loads of old apartment blocks, most of them about twenty years old.

Limassol really began to be born after the Greek Cypriots were thrown out of the North in 1974 by the Turks. A large majority of them came over to Limassol and started to develop it as their second main city after Nicosia. However, none of this changed the fact that in the immortal words of U2, "we still hadn't found what we were looking for!"

As we continued to search we noticed that some properties were being sold with title deeds and some without. Like most foreigners we didn't really pay much attention to this minor detail. We only came to understand its true meaning later after further investigation. The Estate Agents certainly didn't pay much heed to it and were clearly happy to sell non title deed properties along side properties with title deeds. Before I go on let me first give you these words of advice, "Do Not Buy Property Without Title Deeds!" It's very simple but something that many foreigners don't realise. Quite simply, if the property does not have title deeds, you or the so called current owner does not own it. The title deeds are proof of ownership, proof that the property has been registered with the land registry. Without them the true and rightful owners- in an apartment block this could be the people who own the actual land, not the individual apartment- could pop up at any time and claim back their property leaving you up the creak without a paddle. As I said, do not buy property without title deeds.

Amazingly, many foreigners are continuing to do exactly that and some have already been caught out. The mad thing is that the agents are still selling these properties at the full market value as ones with title deeds. This is because people are still not aware of the real implications and as I said the good old Estate Agents aren't about to tell them when their 5% is at stake.

In the Paralimni/Agia Napa end this has been a real problem that has just recently come to the forefront, as the Old Mayor and other officials were being taken to court for corruption. Basically they were being paid off by frustrated developers so that they could be granted permission to build quickly, rather than having to go through the whole lengthy procedure of obtaining the correct permits, which they might not have been granted and subsequently never been issued title deeds for the apartments they were selling.

As we looked at more and more apartments it was clear that although they were only twenty years old, which in English terms is not that long a period of time, in Cypriot terms that is an eternity. Most of the buildings were in a terrible state. This southern side of Cyprus sits on what's known as the Cypriot Arc. This is a fault line that arcs through Paphos around off the shore of Limassol. What this means is that Cyprus, particularly the southern side is prone to small earthquakes and as you can imagine over the years, what with the, shall we say, not best of constructions, has taken it's toll on the buildings.

Despite this, surprisingly enough from our experience, the thing that has caused more damage over the years to these buildings is not the might of nature, no, it's the people themselves! They have simply never maintained their buildings. They do not seem to appreciate the importance of maintenance and as a result have let many of these buildings fall apart. Many of them have been renting out their apartments and simply refuse to pay maintenance, or common expenses as it is know in Cyprus, even though they are charging their tenants for this. They have no issues with renting out their apartments with damp, poor plumbing and water tanks that have been rusting away for years, open to the elements with stagnant mosquito infested water that stinks.

The tenants are unwittingly using this polluted water to wash with, unaware of the obvious health implications. Also, the roofs are notoriously bad! Not just the old ones, but on the new buildings as well. It seems to be a standing joke here that everybody's windows or roof leak. Not so funny when it's yours and your apartment is constantly filled with a musky damp smell that refuses to vacate, even throughout the eight or so months that it doesn't rain. As I just said, fortunately it doesn't rain so much out here but don't let that fool you, because when it does rain, boy does it rain. And afterwards, if you've picked a top floor apartment as we did, you'll be the one who's up on top of the roof mopping! Believe me after the first hour of mopping the view from up there doesn't seem to be quite so amazing after all.

Cracks come as standard but it's an extra for all the exterior rendering to be falling, or have fallen off, exposing the bare walls and the steels.

After careful consideration the apartment we finally chose had pretty much all of the above, but none of that mattered because all the external building works were in the process of getting done. At least that's what the Estate Agents told us, and what possible reason would they have to lie? We were fed the old line, as all the foreigners are who don't know any better, that all these buildings are slowly being brought up to EU standards- that there are new government programs in place to assist and give financial grants towards it. They made it sound so easy, as only an Estate Agent can.

Well... this building that we were interested in was definitely in serious need of a makeover but it was in a great location and had a fantastic sea view, which, after all, is all us stupid tourists want! So we thought that if, as our friend Jed the Estate Agent just told us was true that this building was indeed about to get fixed, it would be a good investment. It would, after all be worth far more when all the works had been completed. We just wanted to be sure so we cleverly, or so we thought, went back to the building and grabbed one of the residents to ask the million dollar question. Are all the works here really about to get done? The answer, from who I now know to be Demis, was happily, "yes".

Great you would think. There was just one problem. It was a serious misunderstanding of the Cypriot mentality coupled with an unlucky pick of people to ask on our part. You see, despite never wanting to maintain their buildings or pay anything towards their repair, when confronted with such questions they will always reply with the most positive answers. Like fools deluding themselves from the truth of their own situations. Also to make matters worse, Demis turned out to be one of the few residents who really wanted these works to happen and was happily holding onto the thought that they might. The truth as we later found out was that they were not. It was yet another rouse that the Estate Agents will use to get the sale and their 5%. Yes, whilst it was true that there were grants available to get these buildings repaired, the reality of getting one was entirely another story. As far as the residents being in the process of getting together to repair this particular building, well that was an out and out, dare I say, lie!!! I'll go into that story later. Anyway after confirmation from Demis we were happy with our choice and put in an offer which was duly accepted. As always the thousand pounds deposit was taken off us and we were raced in to see the solicitors to finalise the deal.

They were a firm called Grupianou. A firm recommended by Fuller and based in Limassol. It was like walking into the set of Ally McBeal. This was woman power gone mad and power dressing that made Dynasty look mild. The office was almost entirely run by women which in Cyprus is quite amazing. It was neat and tidy, almost clinical. Everything was neatly stacked in its rightful place and every desk had its own flat-screen monitor to accompany its own computer. It was an office clearly well organised by women with a few carefully picked fresh flowers carefully placed in a couple of the corners. Their perfume wafted around the office like a dream - a permanent reminder to us men as to who really runs the show.

The preliminary documents for both our off plan apartments and the resale were drawn up for us to look at. Also, the main objective here was for them to get us to sign power of attorney over to them. This is something that you hear loads of horror stories about. People signing their whole lives away, being conned and finding all their bank accounts cleared and properties transferred out of their names. Well whilst it's true you must be careful, in fact it is something that is worth doing in order to help things run smoothly if you are not planning on being in the country very often. The thing to make sure of is that the Power Of Attorney is drawn up specifically only to cover the said business in question and nothing else. The other thing is that before any decision can be made, or documents signed on your behalf they must first of all inform you and get confirmation that it is O.K for them to proceed. If the P.O.A you're being asked to sign does not stipulate these things then seriously think twice about signing it!

In fact Martina from Grupianou was fantastic. Professional and efficient something that sadly can not be said for all of the solicitors in Cyprus as we later found out. With P.O.A signed we flew back to England the proud owners of two new builds and one resale two bedroom apartment in Cyprus. We were happily oblivious to the problems that we were going to be forced to face. Unaware of the stress that lay ahead of us. We had quite enjoyed our weeks stay in Cyprus. It had been extremely hard work but very productive, or so we thought!

CHAPTER 4

Back For More

The next few months that followed were strange. We couldn't seem to get Cyprus out of our heads. We had had just about enough of our stress filled jobs. Having to work every hour god sends for ungrateful people, and as for the ever increasing cost of living, making a change seemed more and more appealing by the second. Lara hated, with a passion, the daily toil of her rush hour Northern Line tube journey. A journey that she had to endure every day just to make it to her dungeon of an office where the only natural light to be seen was from the fading memory in her mind. Here all she had to look forward to was a long day chained to a computer and the same soul destroying journey back home by which time all she felt like doing was crashing out ready to begin yet another day of drudgery.

I, on the other hand, was self employed and ran my own little electrical/telecoms business. A business that was getting increasingly more stress full by the day, with ever changing technologies and customers requirements getting increasingly more complex. Everything was a matter of life and death. Everyone wanted it now and everyone wanted it cheap! I found myself forever racing against time, feeling like the bloody white rabbit. Leisure time was at an all time low and stress levels were at an all time high. It sparked the question, was this how life should be? Eventually we both came to the conclusion that the answer was,

"No!" Life was definitely not meant to be like this. As well paid as our jobs were, the stress and time were just too high a price. So it was on a dark dreary English evening before Lara was due to fly to Edinburgh again with her work, when I raised the question, "Why don't we just move over to Cyprus?" It was meant to be one of those things people always say or talk about on dark dreary evenings just to create conversation, but never actually to seriously do. To my shock, Lara turned around and replied, "Yeah. Let's do it!"

Worst of all she was dead serious. She was so fed up with her job that she was ready to give it all up. To be fair, I had been quizzing Lara for years about moving to Spain and she had always said "No – what will we do?" However, we were ready to start a new life and a new adventure. So why not Cyprus? I mean we already had our apartment out there, mortgage free. So in that moment of spontaneity and complete madness we both agreed, we'd do it. We'd go to live a new stress free life in Cyprus. A place where the sun shines, the air's clean, the sea's warm, cost of living's lower, the sky's bluer and the grass is greener. At least that's what it said in the brochures and they surely can't be wrong! Can they???

We had already booked tickets back out for January. We were meant to go and kit out our apartment ready for renting but instead we decided to get it ready for us to live in. We decided that we would try renovating old apartments and reselling them just like on the TV shows. We had already done two in England. My first flat and then our house so we had an idea of what we were doing on that front, and we both enjoyed it. Transforming rundown properties into fabulous new homes fit to live in, so it was a complete change of plans. This time we'd be looking for our first renovation project to do for when we finally moved out, which we both agreed would be in May/June giving Lara time to work her notice etc.

As we weren't sure how renovations would pan out, we also decided to get some smaller apartments to rent out. The idea was to spread our investments between new builds, renovations and rentals, and then once over there to decide which one we wanted to focus on. It all sounded great. It was a definite plan and if nothing else, an adventure that would break up the monotony of life. Life's all about adventure and new experiences after all. We dreaded being like most people, going through life never actually doing, and ending up with a fist full of regrets. Our parents thought we were absolutely crazy but as we explained to them, if things didn't work out we could always come back. We were young enough, and ugly enough, to recover and start again if necessary. Not only that but it seemed a good time to go as property prices in England had stopped shooting up. That meant that if things didn't work out we should be able to afford to buy back in England, about where we left off. That was our theory anyway and it made perfect sense to us at the time!

January was actually pretty cold in Cyprus. It was not the scorching place that we had left. You needed a heater at nights and the mornings were bitter. This was the start of the rainy season so the damp spot on the ceiling of our apartment was really coming along nicely. I swear it was growing a beard. This time we had two weeks and as I said our objectives were to get a good first project for when we moved out in May and to get a couple of good rental apartments sorted out. In addition to all these, Lara's parents had bought into the dream too and had asked us to keep on the look out for a small holiday apartment for themselves. I'm not sure whether we were quite qualified to do this for them but we agreed nevertheless! With all these to do two weeks just didn't seem enough time. This time round we wanted to look down on the other side of the island in Agia

Napa and Paralimni where my friend was. We were told that they had the best beaches down that end. That much was not a lie. However, this time of year it was as dead as a dodo in Agia Napa where Jed, our friendly agent, who as you know always had our best interests at heart had some, I quote him, "Excellent investment opportunities for the buy to let investor." Hmm!!!

CHAPTER 5

Buy To Lets

Like little naive children, we listened and absorbed every fact and figure that Jed skilfully fed to us. In fact we scribbled them all down in a note book so as not to forget them. We were definitely interested in the studio apartments using a mortgage to purchase them, so as to spread our money even further. It was easy. Jed had already done the math and had a bank at hand who he recommended could get us the mortgage we needed. They were apparently the very first bank doing Euro mortgages in Cyprus, with no repayment penalties and far lower rates than any of the other banks could offer us, according to Jed!

Ned's figures were as follows. A guaranteed 20 week season at £200 CYP a week per apartment. That's right, you heard it correctly, a 20 week season, guaranteed and yes, CYP not Sterling. That would work out at £4000 CYP income from each studio a year, not to mention the off season lower rate rentals you were, according to Jed, bound to pull in. And these were Jed's "reserved figures". Fantastic!!! Of course there were your expenses i.e. 20% management fees, if required and £200 CYP a year advertising fees. Also, dare we forget, the mortgage. Jed's mortgage worked out at approximately £3600 CYP a year on a £40000 CYP repayment mortgage, decreasing, over 15 years. Still fantastic! It meant that we should have seen, according to Jed's figures, approximately £4200 CYP profit every year. In the immortal words of the Crankies, "Fandabydosee." The only problem was, as we later found out, it must have been the Crankies who pulled these figures out from the air. I think a couple of the requirements needed to become an Estate Agent are a good imagination and the ability to deliver lines. Jed had both these skills in abundance. So like crazed monkeys we took two! We almost went for three ☺

Now where shall we start with these then? As we discovered when we actually started to rent these two apartments out, Jed's figures and theories on rentals were so unbelievably wrong it was frightening! This is the reality. Jed's 20 week season turned out to be, in Agia Napa a 12 week peak season if you're lucky. In fact Agia Napa has experienced a severe year on year drop in holiday makers since all the bad media coverage in 2001. It would be fair to say that the Garage Music scene killed it! As a result the competition in renting apartments in this area is fierce! Basically, the supply is outweighing the demand and the result is prices are low. In peak season £200 CYP per week was the absolute maximum we could get, but it was so rare that we ever managed to achieve it, that it's really not worth talking about. Most of the people who enquired were looking for deals, cheap deals. Those who did book tended to want to book them out for more than one week. In order to compete, we were forced to give discounted rates for these people. If we didn't reduce our rates, we quite simply would not have rented them out at all.

We did pull in a few weeks' rental during the winter, but not enough to make a real difference. We managed and cleaned the properties ourselves, so we didn't incur any maintenance costs, however, the other expenses you've got are the electricity and believe you me, air con units can consume loads. As we found out, when people are on holiday, they will quite happily leave these on all day long just so that when they come back from the beach the apartments are nice and cool. This drinks the electricity like water. You've only got to have a couple of people like this and your bills can sky rocket through the roof. My advice is get a pay as you go air con. You've also got water bills, refuge and advertising bills. We found that our trips over to Agia Napa to clean out the apartments from Limassol were costing us loads of money too in petrol, let alone the wear and tear on our car and our time and effort.

After all of this it turned out that our rentals weren't even covering our mortgage, let alone giving us the £4200 CYP per year profit that Jed had assured us we would make! They became more trouble than they were worth. The obvious option was to sell. The only trouble was that it was so obvious that everyone in our apartment block suddenly had their own apartments up for sale at the end of the first season. So we decided that selling at that time probably wasn't such a good idea. We were stuck with them, like it or lump it. Maybe next year would be better?

While I'm on the sticky subject of buy-to-lets, here's a few more facts and lessons that we learnt about it which the Estate Agents definitely won't tell you. We hope you'll find them interesting...

Did you know that when any foreigner buys a property in Cyprus they must obtain permission from the Council of Ministers to have the property registered in their names i.e. for the transfer of the title deeds? However, the terms of the transfer are that the property is for your private secondary residence only, and you are specifically not allowed to rent it out to tourists. Apparently this is designed to protect the Cyprus tourist industry i.e. the hotels etc. A severe irony you might be thinking since most of these very properties are being sold and marketed specifically to the foreign buy-to-let investors. There is an upside to this. You can let to permanent residents of Cyprus... as long as they're not on holiday. The major down side is that the contract you've just got your tenant to sign is about as useless as a Cypriot committee. Trust us we know, but we'll talk about committees later! For all the above reasons your contract will never stand up in a Cypriot court, just don't let your tenant know that.

If you have a potential long term rental, e.g. for a year, make sure you get as much money up front off the tenant as possible. Most people say at least 3 months rent but I would recommend more if you can. The reason for this, as we found out, is that there are a lot of blaggers out there who will tell you that they want to book for a year in order to get a cheap deal off you. They never have any intension to stay the whole year but just want to get the apartment cheap over the peak season. Then once the peak season is over they'll be off back to wherever they came from leaving you short changed. Obviously the peak season is when you're going to be able to charge the most, and you only give cheaper rates on long term rentals because they will be renting the apartments over periods that you would otherwise not be able to rent out so it evens itself out.

Make sure you compile an inventory and get a security deposit off everyone who rents off you. No matter who they are, or claim to be, even if they're a high up official from the Cyprus government itself. Yes, that's right, it's true. We actually had a member of the Cyprus government renting one of our apartments for a month. I'll name no names but just let me reiterate one more time, *get a security deposit off everyone*, no matter who!

If you're considering attempting to do this from another country my advice to you is, don't. Especially if you're going to entrust an agent with your keys! Bad move! You'll be ringing them up enquiring how the apartments doing and they'll be telling you how unfortunately it's not been renting out too well. When the truth is, they've been renting it out at a low rate without ever telling you, banking all the cash for themselves. Again guess what? Yes, that's right, we've got a personal tale to tell

PETE THENSHORN

about this one as well. Yes, this crap actually does happen for real, but again I'll save that one for later! I think this is buy-to-let information overload! But really, you just can't trust anyone other than yourselves to look after your own properties. Well that's what we reckon! Anyway back to the story...

Whilst over Paralimni end we also found a really nice little one bedroom apartment in Kapparis just outside Agia Napa and past Protaras. Lara's parents had asked us to keep our eyes peeled for something for them. This was perfect. For once with this property everything was good. The building was good and the apartment was good. Too good to be true you're probably thinking. It had parking and was within their budget. So, without delay we put an offer in which was duly accepted. With yet another property under our belts it would be fair to say that we were at this stage going property mad!!! However with this one at least we only had ourselves to blame if it all went pear-shaped!

24

CHAPTER 6

Our Project

Now with our two magnificent rental properties under our belts and Lara's parents apartment secured, all that was left to make this another successful trip was to find our first renovation project. This was to be the one that would keep us busy when we arrived for good in May. We were looking for an apartment that had something special to it but in need of serious renovation. Of course it needed to be at the right price so that there was a decent profit in it for us, and also leave us with enough money to live on for the year. And as if that wasn't hard enough we only had a week left in which to find it. With two days to go this was proving to be more difficult than we had first thought. It's far easier to find these types of properties and get them at a good price when you're not in a rush. You really need to be living in a country with your ears to the ground and eyes wide open to find them. However, luckily for us help was at hand in the form of, yes that's right, you guessed it, Jed. Our very own fairy god Estate Agent. What a guy!

It was described to us as a top floor penthouse apartment with amazing sea views, in need of some modernisation. The apartment was in Limassol and Jed had just got the keys. So without haste we all made our way over to check it out.

It was actually on the eighth floor of a building called Titanic. A building that now holds a special place in our hearts!

The building itself was on the other side of the main road near the old port, and was directly opposite the sea. It had clearly seen better days! Built in 1985 it was in desperate need of some paint. We made our way up to the eighth floor in the one grubby lift that fed the entire block. But it worked so that was a good sign! As we entered Jed warned us to prepare ourselves. To say that this apartment was in need of modernisation, was a monumental understatement.

Virtually all the ceiling plaster had fallen to the floor. The water was actually dripping through onto the floor below, which was forming a rather large green puddle. As a result, the ceiling steels above were exposed and rusting. The roof to this apartment was clearly not doing its job, and judging by the damaged caused and the stench, it had not been functional for years. There were severe cracks in all of the walls and a huge crack across the middle of the floor which acted like some sort of dividing line between the North and the South! The bathroom suits had clearly never been used and were of an era long since forgotten. They were of a lovely bogey green colour. To be quite honest, I could not have imagined that this colour could ever have been in vogue. Well... possibly if you were high on the hallucinogenic drugs of the seventies.

The ceilings were pretty much the same throughout, and the kitchen still had the original brown units and stainless steel sink, once again never used. When we opened the door to the kitchen balcony we were greeted with a pile high load of pigeon shit that coated it like icing. Not nice and most definitely not sweet! On top, sure enough, the roof was completely shot. It was virtually the bare concrete, with only a few bits of flaking off asphalt scattered around. The last remaining survivors from a long drawn out battle against the elements! The water tanks, not only for this apartment but for most of the others, were disgusting! Old rusty tanks that were now completely exposed to the elements and full of stagnant water, most of which were leaking directly onto the exposed roof. English Health and Safety would have had a field day here!

As if all this wasn't enough, the roof had clearly been doubling up as the resident's local dump for years. It was stacked up with filthy old mattresses, armchairs, broken bikes and old satellite dishes to name but a few things. And when I say satellite dishes I don't mean the small ones you see on people's walls. No. These ones, there were two of them, were like the type you get at the airports or on military bases. They were huge and stood dormant, unused, like monsters. There were also fridges, TVs, kettles, toasters and of course lets not forget the, yes you guessed it, the cuddly toy! It was like the bloody generation game on top of that roof, we were the contestants and our Bruce was Jed.

This apartment needed to be completely gutted from top to bottom. It needed everything replacing, windows, tanks, new roof laid, plumbing, electrics, kitchen, bathrooms, ceiling, and steels to be treated. Everything! It was perfect ☺. You see, despite all of the above, the one outstanding feature this apartment had was one of the best sea views I have ever seen. The view spanned across from the front lounge to the front bedroom, and from floor to ceiling. It had a huge size balcony from which to enjoy it and because this building was virtually right on the sea front, it was as if you were on a ship. It was absolutely awe inspiring. It was like an ever changing picture that filled every crevice of the room with light and colour. To all intents and purposes it was to us, blinding!

Like moths to the light we were already sold! Jed didn't even need to give us all his schpeil, but in true Jed style, he went on to do so anyway. I think he couldn't help himself. He told us that the owner was an Arab guy who had bought this property from new and had never lived in it. That much was true. The Arabs had brought up loads of these type properties back in the eighties, and as Jed said, had never even lived in them. What Jed didn't tell us was that they also had never paid, or were interested in paying, any maintenance for them. This is one of the reasons why the buildings have got in such a bad state. When you've got a number of these properties being owned by such people, it makes it virtually impossible to collect enough money in for the general maintenance that needs to take place every year, especially on buildings by the sea.

Jed also told us that this apartment came with parking. This was a plus, we thought. It's always good to have an allocated parking space after all. It also makes a difference to 1) the amount you pay for it, and 2) the amount you sell it for. So obviously, it's extremely important to know what you're buying. At this stage we didn't know the price of builders in Cyprus. I mean, in total this was only our third week of ever being in the Country but luckily Jed had already done some figures! He told us that you'd have to allow a budget of about twenty thousand ponds to do it all up and that we could resell it for about £95k CYP. Jed said that this one was a sure fire winner. The way he spoke it was going to be a nice easy twenty thousand pounds profit.

Oh if only it were that easy! Of course, as always, he neglected to mention the transfer fees of 5% over fifty thousand pounds, the solicitor's fees for purchase as well as sale, the all important Capital Gains tax on profit of twenty percent, and of course, last but not least the Estate Agent's commission of five percent upon sale plus VAT. After you have deducted all of those things your twenty thousand pounds profit soon evaporates away in the heat of the Cyprus sun. Of course, at this stage, we, like many others were not considering all of the hidden costs. The asking price was £60k CYP, a bit high we thought considering all the work that was needed, but as I said we were sold.

This one was going to really stretch us to the limit, so as much as we loved it, we didn't want to pay any more than £50k CYP. We were going to have to take out a loan back in England for this one, but we figured we could pay it off as soon as we sold our house there. Jed put the offer to the Arab. In the end we got it for £55k CYP, a bit more than we had hoped for, but nevertheless we were really excited about the prospect of our first project. Our first ever penthouse apartment.

This time instead of Martina, Jed advised us to go with a lawyer called Pablos who had a small firm in Larnaca. His reasoning for this was that he was more personal and gave a better service at better rates. He also dealt more with properties over the Paralimni side of the island which is better for the Agia Napa studios and Kapparis apartment which we were also purchasing on this trip, so they may as well deal with the penthouse in Limassol too. More like Jed was getting some sort of commission for every client he passed onto this guy! To be honest, we had no complaints with Martina but stupidly we thought we'd give Pablos a go, on Jed's advice.

Big mistake! As they say "if it ain't broke don't try to fix it!" Unlike Martina's office Pablos's office was a complete mess. In place of a computer, folders and papers stood like mini replicas of the leaning tower of pizza on his desk. The floor surrounding it wasn't much better, with books and yet more paperwork scattered like confetti across the floor. It stank of stale smoke and B.O. Clearly there was no woman's touch going on here! In hindsight we should have turned around and walked straight back out of the door then and there and back to Martina. Stupidly, we didn't.

Once again the P.O.As. were drawn up, which to our surprise, were unbelievably long winded compared to Martina's. It wasn't as specific as Martina's either. This, he assured us, was normal which we knew wasn't as we had already had Martina's, but we let him carry on nevertheless as he came on good recommendation. The number of copies he was making was ridiculous. About six, all of which incurred stamping fees. Whilst these fees aren't huge they were unnecessary. Martina only ever needed to do about two copies and maybe a photo copy if needed not original copies. But we went through with the motions, and left Pablos to deal with the purchase of these properties and in control.

We flew back to England, once again, feeling as if we had successfully achieved everything we had set out to achieve. The foundations for our new life in the sun were laid. Only time would tell if they were solid or of Cypriot build quality...

CHAPTER 7

Bad Omens

Soon after we had arrived back in the U.K. we had a call from Pablos. Well it was actually his fiancée, Maria, who was dealing with our cases. It turned out that she was actually dealing with most of the property contracts. Pablos was actually a criminal lawyer who it appeared had only just started to take on property contracts. She was ringing to inform us that upon further search, it appeared that our penthouse didn't come with allocated parking after all. Naturally we weren't too pleased about this discovery. As a result we tried to negotiate the price down further, but despite this, the Arab wasn't prepared to drop. As annoying as this was, we decided the apartment was still worth it, so we continued with the deal.

In the months that followed we were really busy, working out designs and plans for our first project. We had it all planned out. We brought pretty much everything we needed in England. The bathroom suite and taps off eBay, the entire kitchen from MFI in the sales. Not just one of them, but two of them, one for each flat. The leather corner sofa from DFS in the sale, and let's just say that we were Ikeas best customers. The great thing for us was that Ikea had not made it's way over to Cyprus yet so we were able to completely Ikea the place out without anyone ever knowing. Not that Ikea's a bad thing, just a bit, dare I say, common. You know what it's like. You buy a great Ikea print and the next thing you know, everybody's got it like a rash. Well not a problem for us in Cyprus. This type of modern designer furniture in Cyprus is still loads of money. Of course, when Ikea finally does make it over, all that will hopefully change.

All of that, together with the contents of our house, pretty much filled up the entire shipping crate. The last thing to be squeezed, and I do mean squeezed in, was our super king sized mattress. We knew our exodus was for real when the crate doors were finally heaved shut, and the clang of the iron lock was rammed securely into place. As it was driven off down the road, destination Cyprus, we were only too aware that there was no going back. The wheels were now in motion and gathering speed like a runaway train. A train that we would be following in a week's time.

May 31st 2005, the day of our emigration. It was a typical cold grey May morning and judging by the look of the skies, there was a storm brewing. You could feel the electricity in the air. Lara had spent ages the night before upgrading, and getting our laptop fully functional ready for our trip and our first few weeks before the crate was to arrive with all of our main computers. She made sure it had all of the essentials that we needed to run our business such as wireless internet access, this was a real necessity for us as we lived off the internet corresponding to all our various contacts via email. It also had the usual essentials like our Outlook, which contained all of our contacts, Word, and naturally, a DVD player. This was to be a real essential since we would have no TV either. It was a serious state of the art piece of kit, that is until… lightning struck! I shit you not. Sometimes fact is stranger than fiction. A bolt of lightning shot down from the heavens and frizzled this state of the art laptop like toast. It was rendered completely useless! In the unforgettable words of Victor Meldrew, "I don't bloody well believe it!" Neither could we! Our entire system, contacts and all were wiped out in the blink of an eye. All Lara's hard work, blitzed!

Thankfully, Lara had made plenty of backups, so at least our information was not lost, but the laptop was completely shot. More superstitious people might have said it was a sign, or dare I say, a bad omen! Well, if nothing else, it was bloody unlucky and with only hours left before we were due to fly out, it was too late to do anything about it. We were fresh out of time so we packed up the last of our belongings minus one laptop into our suitcases and made our way to the airport.

The plan was to arrive at Heathrow with plenty of time to spare. Plenty of time to check in and then say our goodbyes. It was as per usual a plan that in theory sounded great, but in actual fact, went completely pear-shaped. The trip to Heathrow was the worst I have ever experienced. The traffic was horrendous. It was caused by major road works being carried out on the M25. No surprise there! As the minutes raced faster than we did, panic began to set in like gangrene. The atmosphere in the car was dire. To make matters worse, due to a detour, we missed our turn off. We had to go all the way to the next junction before we could finally turn back.

We arrived at Heathrow with only 1 hour to spare and absolutely stressed. Check in was no easier. With the check in staff obviously pissed off that we were so late and not the recommended two hours before, it was all we could do to get them to actually check us and our suitcases in. The hand luggage was yet another problem. Our 5kg limit was in excess by 10kg and their stone cold faces told us that they were clearly in no mood to let us off. We had to frantically empty out our bags to make the weight. Finally, we were checked in but after all of that there was no time for long goodbyes. So much for our great plan! We raced through the gates and onto the plane with only minutes to spare. At least that ordeal was over, we had made it. After all of that what else could possibly go wrong?

Well the flight over was a rocky one to say the least, and three quarters of the way there Lara was taken ill. She began to have chronic stomach cramps coupled with feverish shivering and an extreme headache. As if that wasn't enough on decent she began to throw up. By this time we were really starting to think that someone up there was desperately trying to tell us something. This was like something out of a horror, usually when some poor sod comes face to face with evil! Thankfully the plane landed safely in Cyprus.

The way things were going, I was beginning to expect the worst. Lara was rushed to the airport doctor who examined her and amazingly could not find any obvious cause for her symptoms. He gave her some tablets and we made our way out of the airport and to our new home, our two bedroom apartment in, Germasogeia, Limassol. We had got our mate Jed to order a bed for us about a week before, and had some sheets in our suitcases. By the time we finally made it to the apartment we were ready just to crash. How, I don't know, but made it we had. I think most people would have taken the hint at the lightning strike but not us! It would take more than a few bad omens to ruin our plans. This was our new life in Cyprus and we were determined to make it work no matter what!

CHAPTER 8

Jed's Bed

Unbeknown to us at this time, like all good horrors, this was just the part where you think it's all over but then suddenly the psychopath killer suddenly comes to life again and goes on his second blood fest. Well that night, we possibly had the worst night's sleep we had ever had in our lives. For a start the bed that Jed had kindly purchased was a creaker! You know the type, creakier than the floorboards of an old house. If you moved it creaked. If you turned it creaked! Even if you so much as breathed it creaked. We dared not do anything else in it for fear the neighbours would call the police for disturbance of the peace! And to add insult to injury it was tiny! Now I'm not a tall guy buy any stretch of the imagination, but what with the wooden end of the bed protruding above the mattress level I had to have my head tight against the headboard just to squeeze in. For me this was a nightmare, since I like to have my feet over the end of the bed when I sleep. A weird idiosyncrasy, I know, but with this bed that was out of the question.

The mattress was as lumpy as school custard. I can honestly say that this was the poorest excuse for a double bed I have ever had the misfortune to come across. Jed had picked a right one here! At about three in the morning we were awoken by our new piss-head neighbours who were having one of those piss-head rows as only piss-heads can. The sort that has no rhyme or reason. Kicking their door in and screaming at the tops of their voices. We had to call the police out in the end by which time it was about 4:30am.

At about 5:30am, we were once again awoken by what was going to be the daily stereophonic cries of the cockerels. And I do mean cockerels plural, as there was an army of the f**ers out there. It would always start with one of them, the leader we called him, who would call out to the others "cockadoodledoo!" This cry was soon answered by every one of the little cocksuckers from miles around. The trouble was that once you were tuned into the cockerels cry that was it. You couldn't help but hear it.

They finished as they always did, at about 6:30am, giving us a massive half an hour's peace before the grand finale! You know I said we called Cyprus the building site of the world? Well it was at 7:00am when we realised that we were right in the middle of one. Directly outside our window on the other side of the road to our apartment, they had just started to build a house. The diggers were digging, concrete was being poured, the cement machines were turning and the builders were building. Making noise as only builders and dustmen are capable of making. It was like being in an episode of grand design but being unable to turn it off. The upside was that we learnt more about the construction of a house from start to finish than we could ever have done in college. We watched that house being built from foundations to finish. How lucky we were!!! As you can imagine, we stumbled through our first day in a zombiefied blur, neither alive nor dead just f**ing tired!!! Welcome to Cyprus ☺

CHAPTER 9

Bars, Cars & Tenants

Our first priority was to sort out some transport. We only had the hire car for one week and were keen to pay as little out on hire costs as possible, so finding a vehicle was definitely our next goal. Many of the roads in Cyprus, especially the ones up in Troodos, building sites and leading to some of the beach fronts aren't so good so a high wheelbase 4×4 is a really good thing to have. We also wanted one we could chuck all our tools in whilst doing the renovations, so a 4×4 pickup seemed the best choice. Also with one of those we'd blend in perfectly with our surroundings. You see, in Cyprus, there are more pickups than people to drive them. Everywhere you turn there's a pickup. Also, the driving skills of the Cypriots isn't the best in Europe, so it's always good to be in something big with a lot of metal around you. To be really safe you're probably best to buy a Sherman, then you could shoot the really bad drivers off the road, but alas that wasn't quite practical. No, a 4×4 pickup seemed our best bet. The only problem with pickups in Cyprus is that most of them have been completely run into the ground by builders or the suspension shot by the amateur hunters taking them off road. A good second-hand 4×4 pickup is one of the hardest things to find in Cyprus. It's about as hard to find as a good Cypriot driver. However, it's the best thing to have so the hunt was on, and the clock was ticking.

Our budget was £8k CYP so at least we had more of a choice. We were in two minds as to whether to buy one privately and pay a little less, but take more of a chance, or buy one from a dealer, pay more but get a guarantee. As it turned out our hire car man Demitries knew someone who had one for sale. Cyprus is a funny place like that. Everybody knows someone especially when there's eight grand involved. Demitries was recommended to us by good old Jed. He ran a small, back-street hire car company and his cars, to be honest, were never that great. The last time we were in Cyprus we hired from him- a heap of a Mazda, and this time we had a wreck of a Nissan, but he was at least cheap. He would have been right at home in an episode of Only Fools And Horses. You know the type, as dodgy as a bumper car. I mean anyone who still has a Kevin Keagan perm can't be alright?

"Oh yes my friends. Come with me I take you there. It's an Isuzu 4×4 pickup imported from Japan and has only done 30k. A very good deal my friend." Demitries explained to us.

There's no such thing as a very good deal in Cyprus for people who have only lived here for a day. Demitries kindly took us to see this bargain of a 4×4. True enough, it was an Isuzu but the vehicle had clearly been well used. It was five years old and when I looked at the clock, it registered zero miles. This was not a problem, however, as Demitries went on to explain to us. He told us how the clock had broken and had just been replaced but the mileage was definitely 20k. Hmm... that's funny, we thought. We could have sworn he had told us it had done 30k? We said nothing. Looking at the pedal rubbers, we could see that they were worn through to the metal! Not a good sign! 30k was hard enough to believe on a five year old vehicle, but 20k was ridiculous unless it was some sort of old age pensioner who had brought it, but then again what on earth would a pensioner want with a 4×4 pickup? Perhaps they wanted space to chuck their zimmers who knows?

Anyway, the documents would tell us all we needed to know. Demitries told us that unfortunately, there were no documents with this vehicle but new Cyprus documents were being issued. How convenient we thought! Something to do with the Importation Law. However, Demitries assured us that we could trust him. I mean we were his friends after all! What a load of old crap! I think Demitries must have thought we had just fallen off the last boat! The truth is that in Cyprus, everybody is trying to get their slice of your cash and they don't care how they do it. Beware especially of the ones who call you their friends after only just meeting you.

Needless to say we didn't buy this one. Probably one of our better decisions! Of course Demitries wasn't at all happy when we told him that we weren't interested in his bargain. From then on our "friendship" with Demitries plummeted to an all time low and needless to say we do not use him anymore. Nor would we ever recommend him and his dodgy cars to anyone. Well not to anyone we liked ☺

We saw a few private ones advertised in the local Cyprus Weekly paper, and one of the local Cypriot papers, name I can't even pronounce. Some were completely wrecked, others were in serious need of retirement with mileage in excess of 200k but there was one that seemed O.K, but came with no guarantees. In the end we decided to go with one that we had seen through a dealer. He was an ex-pat who used to be in the R.A.F so dealing with him was a lot easier than with the locals. It was slightly dearer but we got that all important guarantee that I think is essential for peace of mind, especially when you've just arrived in a new country and haven't found your feet yet.

So that was the car sorted and happily for us within the week. Now we had our transport sorted out, we could make our way over to Agia Napa to check out our two studios. I know what you're thinking! You're thinking that this is the part where the car breaks down on the journey over. Well amazingly enough you'd be wrong! In fact, our pickup was probably our least problematic buy ☺. Our studios however, were another matter completely!

One of them had already been rented out one month before to two young girls from Wigan. It was organised through one of the local estate agents called, for arguments sake, Purchase Cyprus. They had managed to book one of the studios out for the whole year, which they assured us was far better for us than short term tourist rentals. The price per month wasn't great compared to short term lets. It only just covered our mortgage but apparently there was less hassle, i.e. no cleaning costs, no changing sheets, no key drop offs and no preparing the rooms for each booking. Also according to them, long term tenants were more likely to look after the properties. As usual it all sounded great, so we agreed for them to let this one out long term and to rent the other one out short term so that we could compare the two at the end of the year, and then decide how we wanted to proceed for the future - long term or short term lets.

Stupidly, the girls were moved in without signing any kind of inventory as we weren't in the country to do one. As if that wasn't bad enough the agency had only taken a mere months rental in advance off them, which they promptly took as their commission, and to compound the matter they had taken absolutely no security deposit from them! At the time we didn't realise the implications, we do now! As I keep saying these Estate Agents do not have your best interests at heart. They only care about their commission and Purchase Cyprus made sure they got theirs straight away.

We now know that you must have a clear inventory, which the tenants sign, to agree that all the said items are there as listed. You must take a security deposit off them, usually, about £100 CYP which is fully refundable as long as everything is handed back undamaged. Also, most importantly of all for long term lets, you must take, if it's a year's rental, at least 3 months rent in advance, but the more the better. In other words they will pay the agreed rental every month until the last three months for which they would have already paid.

You must work it this way to protect you against unscrupulous tenants such as these girls, who never have any intension of staying the whole year. They get the peak months for a long term cheap price then leave you completely out of pocket when they piss off back to wherever they've come from after having a great time in your apartment. This leaves you with only the off peak time in which to let out your property, which is virtually impossible. Beware of these types of tenants. The only real way to sift them out from the sincere ones is to do as I've just said and take the 3 months in advance to be worked as I've explained. The real long term tenants shouldn't have a problem with it!

We also had our first short term tenants coming over in a week's time. They had booked the other studio out for two weeks so we had to get over to make sure everything was O.K. While we were down there, we planned to meet up with my mates Pete and Pam. They were both the same ages as us and like us had moved to Cyprus, only they had moved out six months earlier. Unlike us, they had decided to get into the catering business. They had just opened up a bar/restaurant called the Grissly Goat right in the heart of Agia Napa. They had the crazy idea of serving up gourmet burgers to the Agia Napa massive. Not sure how that was going to go down in an area where cheap kebabs and larger rule supreme, but it would be interesting to see how it all panned out for them and if nothing else at least we'd get some free drinks and the pleasure of Pam's deserts which are the best I've ever had the pleasure of experiencing.

Napa was just over an hours drive away, so we loaded up the pickup to the brim with all the essentials. All the things this baby was designed to carry, pushing it to the very limits of its design specifications. Things such as, lilos, fully inflated of course, swim ware, his and hers, masks and snorkels, the all essential cooler box loaded with ice and drinks, blankets, sheets, pillows, towels etc. etc.!!! It was a beautiful day to travel- blue skies and warm summer sun everything we had desired. Everything we had been longing for, but despite this Napa was dead! Just a few stragglers wandering around. The only difference to it now, rather than in January, was that the stragglers weren't on zimmer frames.

Business first we thought, so we headed straight for our apartments which were up the hill near to the Love Boat club. The one thing I would say is to be very careful when buying in seasonally orientated place such as Agia Napa. Remember that seasons can change everything. What may seem a beautifully tranquil place out of season, can suddenly become the nosiest hot spot in the area. Unbeknown to us, Love Boat turned out to be one of the few all night after hour's clubs. It doesn't even open its doors until 4am at which time every piss-head within a 3 mile radius staggers their way to it. So don't expect any sleep if you're unlucky enough to be in one of the apartments directly along the road outside it. This road is used not only by the piss-heads as they head to and from the club but by the rows of cabbies who line it in wait for their next fares. These cabbies aren't you're educated types who read good books on philosophy or any thing like that. No they like to listen to music. Loud music! The irony is that more noise comes from their car stereos than from the actual club or the piss-heads! So watch out!

The plan was to get the business out of the way first of all. Introduce ourselves to the girls, dump our stuff off in the free studio and then make for the sea and chill for a bit. Later we could meet up with Pete and Pam, and quite frankly get completely wrecked with them at their new bar. For once, we didn't have to worry about driving. We could stagger back to our studio and stay the night there.

Well... as soon as we turned the key to our empty studio and pushed open the door, all those plans were shattered. We opened the door to a heap load of stress. Inside, we found the curtains drawn and the bed filled with a young Swedish couple who were, let's say, right in the middle of things, and were as you can imagine, somewhat surprised to see us peering in at them. I've got to say they weren't as surprised as us!!! This apartment was supposed to be empty. As you can imagine, serious words were exchanged. It turned out that they had been in our studio for over a month. The joke was that they even pulled out a tenant's agreement which they had signed with our names on it. This was for a long term nine month let for £150 CYP per month. Of course we had not signed it because we knew nothing about it.

It was let to them by the developers who we had purchased the apartments from. It was actually the son-in-law of the developers who we later found out had a real good little sideline going on. He was renting apartments out without the permission of the owners. Of course, he had all the keys, and I suppose most of the owners were completely unaware of his little enterprise since most of them were in other countries. This couple had paid him directly. He had even taken them personally to get all the bills registered in their names. The audacity of him was beyond belief!

As you can imagine the stress levels on both sides were sky high. They of course were unwilling to vacate, and we on the other hand needed to get them out A.S.A.P. We had our first short term tenant coming out in less than a week to rent it. These people had already paid for their flights- you can see the implications.

We spent all day arguing the toss with the developers, who seemed to be backing the son-in-law. After much heated conversations, it was agreed that they would shift this couple out to another apartment across the way tomorrow. Who knows whether they had permission from those owners, but at least they would be out of ours. Unfortunately, for us, this meant that we now had nowhere to stay for the night, so back to Limassol it was for us. We'd have to make another trip over in the morning to clean out the apartment. Since pickups aren't the most fuel efficient vehicles, this meant yet more money on fuel. We made sure we got the £150 CYP off them although it hardly made up for all the stress caused.

Needless to say it had taken all the fun out of our first time over in Agia Napa, and our night out on the town was completely ruined. Mind you, we still made time for our gourmet burgers and a couple of Pam's deserts. My advice to you, to avoid a similar situation, is as soon as possible change all your locks. Many of the others in our block were doing exactly that as they were getting wise to what was going on. The apartment was of course left in a complete mess. It needed to be completely cleaned. New sheets and towels and loads of items were missing. But without any inventory ever being compiled and signed, what could we do? Nothing! The two girls in our other studio seemed O.K. but you know what they say, appearances can be deceiving!

Whilst we were over Agia Napa end we took a visit to Lara's parent's apartment in Kapparis. Whilst the sale had gone through O.K we were never given plans of the parking area. As a result we still didn't know where our allocated parking space was. Sure enough when we parked there, we got a note from one of the disgruntled residents telling us not to park in his space. It was clear that we needed to speak to Pablos and find out exactly where our plans were, and what was our space. Plans which should have been provided to us as standard, right at the start, together with the contract of sale.

We had not been happy with his service from back in the U.K. He would never respond to emails, never answer questions and even more worryingly his figures for amounts due, varied from mail to mail. So much for a better personal service! Needless to say, our faith in his abilities was fast becoming extremely eroded. We thought it would be easier to sort out when we were in Cyprus so we had waited until now before tackling the issue. And so began our email tug of war which raged for weeks over this issue as we tried desperately to sort it all out.

His first response was that we had parking space No 26. Well, this was about as much use as a blind judge in a beauty contest, since none of the parking spaces were marked. We needed plans! In his second response, he said that this apartment block didn't have any plans because it was too old a building and that it would take a special search at the land registry office to obtain them, at additional cost to us! This didn't sound right to us. With Martina and our other resale, we received complete plans of the apartment and parking area below, detailing exactly which ones were ours. This came, as it should, as standard with no extra costs to us. Apart from this parking issue, we still had the issue of his varying figures, and now his fees were different to the agreed amounts. It was becoming so confusing with him insisting his figures were correct and us insisting that they weren't. Over the coming months, it became clear that we were not going to sort anything out via email!!! A trip back to his office was going to be required!

CHAPTER 10

Committees

Finally we had the much awaited call from the shipping company to tell us that our container had arrived. With the help of a platform our furniture was delivered safely all the way up to the fifth floor of our apartment and in through the kitchen balcony. Even with the use of our friend's garage it filled our entire apartment, bar the bedroom, from top to bottom. No room to swing a cat, huh, in our apartment there was no room to swing fall stop.

Now everything was over we could start to look into the supposed works that were due to be done on the building. The works that good old Jed had assured us were in the process of getting sorted out. Well it soon became clear that Jed's theory on the said works was about as accurate as his rental figures! The truth was that the works were about as likely to happen as pigs have of flying. "Sigar sigar" was a phrase we encountered a lot of from many of the Cypriot residents when asked about the works. Basically translated it means "slowly slowly". In real terms it means absolutely nothing is happening or likely to happen unless you do it yourself! That pretty much sums up Cyprus. Nothing will ever get done unless you do it yourself so be prepared. Sure enough there were a few residents who wanted these works to be done, one of which was our friend Demis who we spoke to way back at the beginning, but none of them were actively doing anything about it. I think they were hoping for a miracle or something. On further investigation it appeared that one of the biggest problems seemed to be the current committee. They were absolutely useless and corrupt! Yes, we soon discovered the wonders of the Cypriot committee in all of its glory!

In Cyprus every building is meant to have a committee appointed of not less than three and no more than five owners. Their responsibilities are to maintain the building, ensure the bills are paid for all the various common expenses such as, electricity, water, refuse collection, cleaners, lift maintenance and buildings insurance to name but a few. They should arrange for common expenses i.e. maintenance money to be collected off all of the owners every month in order to pay for all of the above and to have a surplus for unforeseen emergencies that could occur.

It all sounds great except, in the case of our building, none of the above was being done! The acting committee consisted of five people, none of which actually lived in the block, all of which were renting out their apartments and all of them with only their own greedy little interests at heart. Mainly to pay out as little money as possible and collect as much rent as possible. The situation with maintenance money coming in was dire. Only a few people were paying none of which were the committee who between them owned about 30% of the block. There was just about enough money coming in to pay for the electricity and water. There was no buildings insurance in place nor any ongoing maintenance program. Between them they had over the years run this building into the ground and quite frankly they could not have cared less! The only thing they cared about was collecting their rents in every month, this they excelled at!

The problem was that legally all works must be arranged through the committee especially works of this size. We tried to call meetings with the committee all to no avail as none of them even bothered to turn up. So it was at this point that we came to the conclusion that the only way forward was to overthrow the existing committee. A coup was afoot and we were the ring leaders. We needed to get armed, armed with knowledge!

On further investigation we discovered that there's actually a whole legal document detailing all of the obligations and rules for committees in Cyprus. It's called "The Immovable Property (Tenure, Registration And Valuation) Law of 1993." It's about 22 pages long but I would strongly recommend that if you are ever in a similar situation you should have a good read through it. We read through it about three times over! It details how to elect committees and more importantly for us how to get rid of existing committees members. As committee members they have a legal obligation to take their responsibilities seriously. They can actually be held personally responsible if they neglect these responsibilities and as a result accidents occur. If so they can actually be sued. The problem is that at the moment no one seems to be enforcing this law and bringing these people to account. I can honestly say that this particular committee had jointly, over the years, run this building into the ground. Nonetheless, the committee members were not solely to blame, although they were certainly setting no great standards to follow. It was many of the other owners who also refused to pay maintenance, seeing no need for it, quite happy to be living in crumbling old buildings that in English standards were complete health hazards!

Believe me, as we began to discover, this very same mentality was repeated all over. Many of the other apartment blocks have exactly the same problems all caused by this mentality. We were not alone! Trying to persuade them that if they just start to maintain their buildings it would not only be good for their living environment but that they would make back the small amount of investment needed with profit in the extra value it would add to their properties was like talking to a brick wall. The only things these people would listen too is legal action. There are laws in place whereby if the building is in serious need of repair and people aren't willing to pay you can get the money off them through the courts. Not ideal by any means but if that was the only way forward then that was what we had to do! I mean, in the state our building was in we would have found it hard to even resell it at the same price we paid for it.

So we really had no choice, but once again to do any of that we first of all had to get rid of the existing committee and re-elect one that had the best interests of the building at heart and since the old committee weren't even turning up for meetings this was proving to be a nightmare. However armed with a newly acquired knowledge we discovered that there is a way around this problem. If you can get over 50% of the owners to turn up and sign a document agreeing to the re-election of a new committee then that is legally binding. So all that was left to do was to call another meeting…

The meeting was set for 7:30pm and like true Brits we were punctual to the minute. Together with our German next door neighbour Aida we sat alone in the Foyer. Of course in true Cypriot style most of the others didn't start to turn up until about 8. By 8:30pm everyone, except of course the actual committee members, were there but trying to get them all to sit down in one place was like herding cattle. They would stand around outside screaming amongst themselves in Greek. Then they'd wonder in, arms flying, voices raised and this was just them saying hello to each other.

All three of us sat in a pool of despair as we watched this completely disorganised mock of a meeting take place. It took the wrath of a German woman, Aida who at this stage was boiling over with rage, to tame the local hoards and bring some much needed German efficiently to bare. Once Aida took control the meeting went pretty smoothly. It was agreed to re-elect a new committee. The question was who? Well unfortunately Aida had to go back to Germany so it needed people who were here and committed. Other than us Demis was the most enthusiastic about the works so he was elected the President. This he accepted reluctantly at first although he soon got into the role, a bit too enthusiastically in fact. But better to have an enthusiastic president than one who doesn't give a damn. I was elected as the treasurer, now all we needed was a third. We wanted it to be another Brit as it was generally agreed that Brits tend to get things done so a lady called Molly was our third. She didn't actually live in the block but was representing 2 old female Cypriots who did and were all keen on the works happening. It didn't really matter much since Demis and I could do most of the arranging.

We successfully got everyone to sign agreement to the new committee. Over 50% so everything was now in order and legal. We had in one final swoop successfully overthrown the existing committee and what more, without any blood shed. That night as we left the meeting there seemed to be an air of confidence about the place for the first time since we had arrived and I think for years. It only lasted for a few weeks after until the realities of just what we had undertaken began to kick in!!!

CHAPTER 11

The Team

One of the most important decisions you can make when starting a renovation project is picking your team of builders. Pick the right ones and they can make the whole project run as smooth as a baby's bottom, but pick the wrong ones and they can quite frankly make it seem like a living hell. This was our next task which is in itself hard enough, but when coupled with being in a foreign country, not knowing anyone and not speaking the language it makes it about ten times harder! We set about the task at hand by first of all buying the Cyprus Weekly which is the local English paper. Inside it has a whole advertising section where all the builders advertise their services. And when I say all, I do mean all, good and bad!

I remember browsing through it making notes of all the numbers whilst sitting on our balcony with Coast FM, the local radio station, on in the back ground. Once I had scoured through that, I picked up the local yellow pages and sifted out a few more numbers from there. With numbers at hand it was time to start ringing and arranging for quotes. How did we plan to pick this 1st division team of builders you might ask? Well quite simply, it was to "use the force," and hope for the best. To be honest that's the way it felt sometimes, but seriously we wanted to get a team of builders together who we felt confident with and most importantly ones we felt we could trust! It wasn't just about the cheapest quote. Also I happened to be a qualified sparkie and have been in and out of sites all my life, so I have a pretty good idea about all of the various trades and how things should be done. I was relying on that experience to be able to recognise the good from the bad. So now it was time to let the games begin. I rang all the numbers and made appointments to meet all the builders. Our good old mate Jed new of some local developers who said they might be able to help us so a meeting was arranged with them too.

After meeting a few of the Cypriot builders it soon became obvious to us that we really needed to pick an English team. We found that the Cypriot builders just wouldn't listen to what we actually wanted. Jed's ones were the worst, no surprise their! They came waltzing in with their wireless headsets glued to their ears like two cy-borgs from an episode of Star Trek. They wouldn't even speak to Lara, I mean she was only a woman after all, and barely listened to a word of what I was saying either. All of our requirements they just fobbed of telling us that that was not the way to do this apartment out. They even had the cheek to tell us that when they do this job we must leave them alone. They suggested that we go away on a long holiday until they'd finished. I've never heard of such nonsense. Then they tried the old scare tactics telling us how hard it was going to be. Even telling me of all people that the electrics would be a big problem which I knew was a complete load of old cack! As I said they were the worst but the other Cypriot Builders weren't much better. The biggest problem they seem to have is that they just don't listen to what you're saying and want to do it their own way, usually the easiest way for themselves not the neatest or best way for you. This of course was not what we were looking for. We needed builders who we could communicate with and who would listen and do what we wanted. The only ones who seemed to be able to do this were the British ones.

Now we had an even clearer idea of what we were after it was time to pick the team. The first and most important member of our team was Del. Del was a stocky expat who came together with his son Carl. They would provide the all important muscle! The general meat and two veg building works that are the backbone of any renovation. They were on the same wave-length as us. Two straight to the point, no messing guys with whom nothing was a problem. They had their own team of immigrant workers and knew the best places to get virtually anything. We made it a point to check out the other jobs that they had done. Their work looked great so they were in. If you're ever having to pick builders I would also recommend that you do make the effort and check out some of their other jobs before you employ them.

Next of all we needed to get this apartment topped out. It needed a new roof so we needed the services of some good roofers. This came in the forms of Martin and Sid. Two expat roofers from Larnaca. Fantastic couple of guys. At first glance it appeared that Martin was born to do roofs. He was a monster of a man at 6ft 6inches tall he dwarfed his partner Sid who was more suited to do drains, at only 5ft 4inches. Sid was as thin as a rake but as strong as an ox. When they were both standing side by side they could have been a comedy duo made in heaven.

Next was the plumber. A man named Pete. Expat white van man always complaining about the type of taps or the type of toilets we had brought but always willing to adapt where needed and always game for a laugh. Electrics myself and apprentice Lara. Interior design Lara and apprentice me. Painting and decorating both Lara and I and believe you me we ended up doing a lot of it. Andreas was the only Cypriot of the bunch and that was because we quite simply could not find any expats who were doing air conditioning units. He was a Manwell of a man, with a short moustache and aged about 55.

Last but least was the one who we called our wild card. We described him like this because we were never quite that sure about him. Our spider senses were tingling when it came to JR and his weird wife. Another bit of advice for you is always listen to your spider senses! JR as he liked to be called was our supposed kitchen fitter/carpenter. He came with all the waffle. According to his leaflet he was a specialist at everything! Particularly, according to him, kitchen fitting and carpentry which was what we needed. We needed someone who could fit flat packed kitchens and once again JR assured us that he had fitted loads of them. Limited by choice we picked him. You see, no one else seemed to want to touch flat packed kitchens. Most of the kitchens in Cyprus are made to measure and built by the carpenters on site at half the cost of ours. Except of course the expensive designer Italian ones, so everyone had great pleasure in rubbing this in. Flat packed kitchens were not the norm. However we had already spent a lot of money on ours so it would have been crazy not to use it. But as I said luckily for us JR was the man who can!

Unbeknown to us he came as a package with his weird wife. We never did catch her name. I think she was Scandinavian or something but we both agreed that she was weird. She arrived with him when he first came to look at the job. Baring in mind this was a building site, she was wearing a long gypsy-type dress and frumpy frock to boot. JR didn't appear much more builder like with his thick rimmed glasses that perched precariously at the end of his long noise. She just stood there with this strange stare and a fixed smile that quite frankly was just not normal! We both thought that it was hardly professional to turn up with your wife to look at a job but as I said we didn't have anyone else so we decided to give him the benefit of the doubt- maybe they were on their way somewhere else or something? She was probably just tagging along for today.

Boy were we wrong! It turned out that she was to be with him every single day. They were a husband and wife combo from hell! However the one thing JR really could do was talk! He could talk the hind legs off a donkey. Not you're interesting type of talk either. No, we're talking about that seriously boring mono droning type of dribble. The unbearable type that you feel you have to escape from or else you'll physically die! When we first met him he would drone on about what a perfectionist he was. His key words were always repeated by his wife in an annoyingly high pitched Scandinavian screech. He told us stories of other jobs that he had been on where he had been called out to fix other builders bad jobs.

My resistance to it was extremely low. I worked out that I could take about two minutes at the most and then I had to get away, even if he was in mid sentence. Lara seemed to have a slightly higher resistance to it. It was a good ten minutes before she had to escape! He had loads of these stories! Looking back we reckon these were jobs that he had messed up, but we'll never know for sure! As I said JR was our wild card and boy did we regret it!

So, finally we had picked our team and now work could commence on our first renovation project. The first of many we hoped.

The roofers worked their asses off for us. They cleared the entire roof of all the junk that had been deposited up there over the years. They ripped out all of the derelict water tanks that had been leaking through our roof, and had been contributing to the massive damage inside. We couldn't have them continue to leak on our new roof otherwise there was the very high possibility that they would leak through again. We had tried to get in touch with the owners of these tanks but all to no avail and the tanks were clearly unused. They were rusted away with stagnant green water, mosquitoes and dead pigeons to name but a few things that were inside them.

Unable to contact the owners, we did however call a man named Kyriacos. A man who we grew to detest with a passion! He was the main man on the building's committee. An old slimy man who was in charge of the building's maintenance, not that you could see any. He was also in charge of collecting common expenses off everyone, this he was very good at!

We showed him the derelict tanks and told him what we intended to do. It was very hard getting through to him, as he would just wonder off every time we tried to talk to him. At this point we gave him the benefit of the doubt and put this down to him not being able to speak very good English. We later found out that he spoke perfect English and was in fact one of the rudest, unhelpful, twisted individuals we have ever had the misfortune to meet!

Anyway after some time he assured us it was O.K to take these tanks away and agreed with us how bad they were. So out they came to make way for our new roof. This was our first problem since no sooner than they had come out we were confronted with our first irate Cypriot. Sure enough one of the owners had been informed, and was now on the roof screaming blue murder. He was nowhere to be found when we tried to contact him before but now all of a sudden he was the most wronged man on the face of the planet. He said he had spoken with Kyriacos who apparently also could not believe what we had done. Well we thought this was strange since we had run the whole thing past Kyriacos before hand. He was threatening to take us to court if we didn't replace his tank with a new one. He wasn't actually living in his apartment, just renting it out, and the water was so stagnant so there was no way anyone could have actually used it. It was outrageous that he hadn't renewed his water tank years ago. It was the same old story, he was quite happy to rent his apartment out knowing that his water tank was a health hazard. Not only that, but it was leaking through our roof. We told him all of this and refused to buy a new tank for him. Needless to say, he wasn't very happy and went off vowing to take us to court. Nothing ever happened. Fortunately he was full of hot air. Later he changed his tank for a nice new one. Something he should have done years ago.

CHAPTER 12

Kilani

Del and Carl were racing through the job like there was no
tomorrow. Just a few of the materials couldn't squeeze in the lift.
So working on the eighth floor hadn't been too much of a problem. They were moving much faster than we had expected. No
real issues there other than the usual few complaints about the
noise. Other than that things were going great. Pete's plumbing
job went really smoothly too. He did love to complain though
but still no real problems. It was clear that we were well on
target for our three month turn around time. With any luck the
way things were going we'd probably have it knocked out in
two. So we decided to put the feelers out for our next project. It
came in the form of a run down old house near Troodos. Within
a beautiful wine producing little village called Kilani. We looked
at pictures of it together with some others in the Estate Agent's
office. It was up for fifty thousand pounds a bit over our budget
but we liked the looks of it nevertheless. When we expressed an
interest in it, the weirdest thing happened. The Estate Agent
started to advise us against even bothering to look at it. He said
it's a terrible property, it needs loads of work. Coming from an
Estate Agent this was very strange behaviour! Despite his best
efforts to put us off we were really keen to see it. They wouldn't
even take us up to see it so a meeting was arranged with the
owner, a man called Maximus!

Maximus was a larger than life character. An ex-army man with a taste for hard licker and gambling. It was his gambling habits that had forced him to sell this property. He told us how the Estate Agents had been terrible, and had not shown anyone his property. Naturally he was not very satisfied with their service, especially since they were charging their 5% commission. The house was just perfect for us. Yes, it needed a lot of work but nothing that couldn't be done- although Maximus was insistent that it was fine the way it was and that a nice young couple like us could move straight in.

It had a huge grape vine that flowed down around it and the smell of pine trees filled the air like wine. The location was excellent, it was hidden away down the end of a small cul-de-sac and the only noise to be heard was the occasional songs from the birds. This was a tranquil slice of paradise and we both fell in love with it immediately. Careful not to show Maximus how much we loved it, we began negotiations. Maximus insisted on negotiating over dinner and drinks, lots of drinks. Of course this put him at an advantage as he could eat and drink us both under the table.

Our negotiations went on for about two weeks until eventually we agreed on a price of forty thousand pounds. Ten thousand below his original asking price. This price, although low, was to absolutely wipe us out. We were using our living money in order to get it and in doing so were playing a mad game of monopoly for real. We had worked out that this deal was going to leave us with just enough money to live on for six months at which time if we hadn't managed to secure a sale on our first project it was going to be game over for us! So now the pressure was really on, and the stress levels were to reach an all time high. Ironical seeing we came to Cyprus to reduce them. Maybe the truth is that if you are that sort of person it doesn't matter where you are in the world. You'll never really be content with just a nice life, you'll always be striving for more and in doing so will create stress for yourself.

Maximus told us that the Estate Agent had offered him forty thousand for his property, but he had refused to sell it to him. The Estate Agent had even told Maximus that if he changed his mind his offer would still stand. Suddenly, it all became clear why the Estate Agent was so insistent on trying to put us off seeing it. He obviously wanted it for himself, and was hoping that Maximus would get so despondent with not getting any viewers that he would let him have it. Well, unfortunately the plan had backfired on him. Indeed Maximus had got despondent and was desperate to sell, but instead of selling to the Estate Agent he had sold to us. A classic case of being in the right place at the right time. We told Maximus how the Estate Agent had tried his best to put us off, and needless to say he was furious! He wanted us to go direct with him for a few grand less so that he would not have to pay their fees. As tempting as this was we refused for fear of backlashes in the future. Unfortunately, you never know who might have your next property or your next buyer. Insistent, Maximus refused to pay the whole five percent and instead gave them three percent telling them that they had not earned it. He also refused to pay the vat they were charging, all fifteen percent of it, and in doing so taught us a couple of very important things that we weren't aware of!!!

The first thing is, that if the "Estate Agent" you are dealing with is not a registered agent, as many of them aren't- and make no mistake we're not just talking about the small back street ones, no, we're talking about some of the biggest ones on the Island, naming no names for fear of possible repercussions. Yes, some of the biggest ones are not registered estate agents - quite simply you will not be able to claim back any of their fees, or the VAT if you are a company, they charge you as an expense to offset against your profit, which in turn will substantially increase the amount of tax you will have to pay if ever you come to resell. In fact, one of the big ones has just won a case in the Cyprus courts to now allow it to charge these fees as "advertising fees" and call themselves an "advertising agency." Although this is a bit strange, at least in this way you can claim back their fees. In our case obviously this was an important thing to be aware of. You see, the government considers any payment of commission made to an unregistered Estate Agent as unlawful hence un-claimable.

This can, as Maximus showed us, be a very useful thing to know in order to negotiate a lower commission rate with them. A rate that would compensate for the money you would lose not being able to claim it back. It does lead to the question of, how can they be charging VAT on commissions that they are not legally meant to be charging? Well I haven't got the answer to that one yet. I can only suppose that there are some fingers being well oiled in high places, but what do I know? I suppose most of the time no one knows about this, especially the foreign buyers so they pay it without blinking an eyelid. I mean, up until now *we* certainly weren't aware about this. My advice to you is ask them whether they are registered Estate Agents and if not give them hell. Get their fees down and do not pay the VAT they are charging!

There was one more thing that we discovered whilst doing our searches on Kilani. This was food for thought! Some of the properties up and around Troodos were previously owned by the Turks as indeed were some of the old colonial wrecks that are scattered around Limassol old town and the surrounding areas- buildings that are now being sold on. Well, we're all aware of the advice telling us not to buy in the North of the island as most of the properties being sold over there are really owned by Cypriots who were forced to leave them behind. My question is this. Surely just as many Turks were forced to leave their properties in the South. So what's the legal situation going to be if you buy one of those? I personally don't know but I reckon it's something to be aware of!

This time needless to say we did not use Pablos and instead used our original solicitor Martina to deal with the purchase. At least we were learning, and now with Kilani under wraps. we could continue with Titanic in the knowledge that our next project was now lined up for us.

CHAPTER 13

Unlucky For Some

The longer we came to and from Titanic, the more we began to realise just what a state it was in. There had clearly been no maintenance going on for years. Simple things like light bulbs not being replaced, lamp covers missing, graffiti, people using the downstairs car park as a dump. The lift had that terrible lingering urinal stench and the letterboxes in the foyer had been repeatedly vandalised. Half of them were completely ripped off and the other half were hanging on to their hinges for dear life. So much for the low crime rate! These are all the sort of things that people, like us, coming over from England are oblivious to. All we see are the amazing views. I mean, when coming over from the grey concrete jungle of the city, it's hard to see anything else. The Estate Agents certainly don't want you to look any deeper. But if you want to save yourself a whole heap of misery, try your utmost to look past the view. Take a good hard look at the building itself. Front to back, top to bottom, inside and out and on every floor. It just could save you a lot of stress and money! Generally it's only after spending some real time in a place that you see past the view, and start to peer a little harder. Suddenly the veil of the view is lifted from your eyes and all the hidden flaws become blindingly obvious.

Naively, we reckoned that most of these problems could be sorted out with a fresh coat of paint. A bit of movie magic! Boy were we wrong, nevertheless it was our intention to fix all of these things. If we couldn't get the committee to do it, we would do it ourselves and look at it as part of the job. If it could be painted we'd paint it. After all, it would all help towards the sale of our property if the exterior appeared to be a bit better.

Things continued to go well on the job. The electrics went in without a hitch and we were well on course for finishing within two months. This would have been a brilliant turn around time and was great for us since it obviously meant more selling time. All that was left now was the kitchen. It was time to see what JR could really do.

JR turned up on time, as planned, closely followed in by his weird wife! Lara and I looked at each other in disbelief. She was still dressed in the same gear, her long gypsy dress and frumpy blouse. However, as I said we needed the kitchen installed and whilst this was a bit unorthodox, we gave them both the benefit of the doubt. It wasn't long though, before we started to have serious concerns about them. In my experience it's always a really bad sign when a tradesman starts to ask to borrow your tools. Especially when the tradesman is supposedly a carpenter and the tools he's asking to borrow are chisels and jigsaws! His freaky wife was sat on the floor in the corner attempting to assemble all the units whilst JR studied the instructions looking rather puzzled. This again gave us both cause for concern. Things went from bad to worse. Everything was a problem for him. He couldn't seem to figure out the simplest of things, from how to fit the worktop to cutting the right size holes in the units for the pipes and wires. It was a real struggle and came to a climax after he arrived back on site following a week's break because he didn't have the right tool for cutting the worktop.

After delaying us a whole week, he then had the audacity to ask for more money because he was going to have to wait an hour for me to move some wires. He had the cheek to say the job was taking far longer than he had estimated for. Well, he stood about as much chance of getting anymore money out of us as pigs have of flying. The only thing he got from us was laid off. Not something that we get off on but in his case it was something that we should have done a lot sooner. His weeks delay had not just cost us time, but more importantly potential sales time. Time our property could have been on the market- a week earlier and who knows, in that week there may have been a buyer. You just never know. In that instance his delay could potentially have cost us a sale. Food for thought!!!

Him and his weird wife left screaming that we'd never be able to get anyone else who could do the job for us. Well JR and weird wife whatever your name is? Just to let you know that we ended up fitting the kitchen ourselves and it really wasn't that hard mate ☺. Fitting the kitchen ourselves was something that wasn't in the plan but something that, at this late stage, we had no choice in doing. In total JR had set us back about two weeks, but despite that we were still on target of meeting our three month turn around time. We had worked our arses off for three months solidly, living off kebabs and tea. Now, finally it was finished and looking absolutely fabulous. The designer look that we and Ikea had created, complemented the unbeatable sea views perfectly. The roof was completely cleared, the rubbish downstairs was cleared, light bulbs and covers replaced and all of the common areas were now free from graffiti and were gleaming with fresh white paint. No thanks to the committee! We had exorcised the lift of all it's fowl odours and lined it with laminate to cover all it's scars. This building looked as if the A-Team had been at it! Well, it did at least on the ground and the eighth floors, no prizes for guessing why only those!

Now, finally, we were ready. Ready to sell this magnificent white elephant of ours! We decided to move ourselves in just until we sold. Might as well enjoy a bit of this luxury that we had created we thought. Just one incey wincey problem. Just after we had moved in and just as we were about to approach the Estate Agents with our wonder, the worst thing happened. The worst thing that is, for anyone trying to sell an eighth floor apartment! Yes that's right you guessed it. The bloody lift broke. No lift equated to no sale. It was as simple as that, and what with our financial situation being as dire as it was this had the potential of being a serious setback! At first we hoped that this was just a standard breakdown, and that the maintenance guys would come out and work their magic on it as they had done in the past. However it soon became apparent that there were more serious problems behind this breakdown! When we spoke to the maintenance company, instead of the usual "O.K., we'll be out in a few hours to have a look at it," all we got was, "Speak to Kyriacos. He knows all about it!" Something was not right.

We tried to ring the elusive Kyriacos, whose phone was now conveniently switched off! It was at this point panic began to set in like gangrene. Our stress levels began to soar. This was one problem that at this moment in time was completely out of our control! Helpless, we continued to try to get to the bottom of this so we rang the lift maintenance company yet again but this time we were put through to the owner. Our worst fears were confirmed. He explained to us that the lift had been switched off by them. The reason for this was that there was an outstanding bill of over four thousand pounds. Our hearts sank as we began to realise the severity of the situation. Apparently the lift had been overhauled about six months ago but to this date the lift company had not received any of the money owed to them for the works. Kyriacos was aware of the situation and had done nothing! All we could do was to keep ringing Kyriacos and see what he had to say on the matter.

You know what they say- that timing is everything? Well as

luck would have it, it was at this exact same time when we had a call from our agent down in Agia Napa, to inform us that our long term rental had just done a bunk and p**sed off back to the U.K without paying their last months rent. These lovely northern lasses had taken us for mugs. They had had four months of the peak season in our studio for peanuts. Boy did we feel like complete and utter muppets! Talk about being kicked when you're down. Well, I felt as if I was being kicked right in the nuts! Needless to say, we were at this stage, at an all time low. We felt as if someone up there was playing a sick and twisted joke and having a good old chuckle at our expense. Things really could not have got much worse and there seemed to be no end to it. No light at the end of the lift shaft. At least not with it being out of order anyway!

We continued to climb up and down those eight flights of stairs for two or three days before we finally got through to Kyriacos. He told us that he had been away but not to worry the problem was in hand. He had broken down each apartment's share of the bill and was going to start to collect it. His master plan for collecting this money was… to put one small sign up on the foyer wall. Call me stupid if you will, but what hope did a piece of paper have of staying up if the wooden letter box doors couldn't even stay up. But he assured us that he would have all the money in by the end of next week.

Well we now know that trying to get maintenance money off people in this country is hard enough let alone a large amount. And this was a large amount, £3500 CYP in total. Stupidly we listened to Kyriacos and waited! Sure enough his feeble notice lasted about a day before it was ripped off the wall in contempt and shredded into tiny pieces never to be seen again. The end of the next week came and went with no change. The best season for selling was slowly slipping away, and with every day that passed without a lift, the disgruntled residents took their anger out on the walls that we had painstakingly painted.

We spoke to Kyriacos again with growing discontentment at his management of the situation. It became all too clear that he really didn't give a damn. I mean after all, he wasn't the one having to climb up and down the eight flights of stairs. He didn't have to live in the block. And for us the cherry on the top of the cake was that we found out that he was actually charging for his fantastic services. He was being paid £150 CYP per month, all of which was coming out of our monthly maintenance money. We caught up with him in the restaurant below Titanic where most nights he and his Butthead friend would sit like kings, drinking coffee. We asked him again what was happening, this time clearly getting more agitated at his lack of results. Yet again, he assured us that he had collected more of the money in, and he expected the rest to be paid by the end of the next week. Exactly how much money he refused to tell us, just instead, sniggering at our questions together with his Butthead friend. He was clearly getting off on our predicament.

We were really beginning to despise him. Once again we waited as he put another sign up on the wall. This one lasted less time than the last. Was he ringing people? No! Was he putting letters in everyone's doors? Who hadn't paid? Half of the people in the block weren't even aware why the lift was not working and the other half didn't care. As illogical as it sounds, they would rather walk up the flights of stairs loaded with shopping than pay towards the lift being repaired. In fact to our shock we discovered that the lift had actually been out of service for a whole year prior to its repair. It took the government to get involved as no one would pay for it to be repaired before. It must have only just been repaired when we first looked at it. Something that good old Jed and his cronies neglected to tell us! If these people had gone a whole year without it working before then what hope had we of them ever paying to get it to work now?

As time went by this became more and more irritating knowing that we were one of the few that had paid. It appeared that it was only a few residents, mainly the ones at the front of the building with sea views, who ever paid for anything. The ones at the back of the building were poorer, mostly refugees renting cheap off uninterested landlords, who never paid for a thing. No chance of getting any money off them, especially with Kyriacos on the case.

By the end of the third week we were pulling our hair out with worry. Every day we were patching up our walls as graffiti began to spread like wild fire. The roof that we had so painstakingly cleared was beginning to get filled up once again with people's crap. First of all a TV and then a mattress. It was like a plague and spreading fast. With the lift out of order the nearest place for people who lived on the top floors to dump was the roof, or if they were too lazy to make the roof, the stairwells seemed to be another favourite! It wouldn't be long before it was in exactly the same state as when we found it.

It was at the end of the third week when we were confronted with the huge words scribbled on the foyer wall in thick red marker pen. There was no poetry in the words that we were facing just utter ignorance. It read, "When's the f**ing lift going to work?!" This was the wall that we had just repainted the day before in an attempt to patch over the graffiti that had been left on it. Our stress and anger were getting too much to contain. Time was running out for us. With only limited finances, no income and being dealt a terrible chance card like the lift we were in serious danger of going bankrupt. We had to do something and we had to do it quickly!

We met up with Kyriacos once more in the restaurant, where he sat together with his side kick Butthead as he always did. Once again he tried to fob us off telling us that he had already collected £1500 CYP. "Sigar, sigar!" he said sarcastically as Butthead sniggered from across the table like some naughty school kid. However, these two idiots were far from kids and this was no joking matter. This was our life! Kyriacos was clearly getting some sort of twisted kicks out of our frustration.

"I should have some more in by the end of next week." He chuckled as he sipped his coffee without a care in the world. From that point on our words became heated. "You keep saying next week!" we yelled at him. "It's not good enough and we certainly can't wait another week for you to continue your feeble attempts at collecting this money." We demanded that he showed us who had and had not paid. This, he again refused to do. Then he had the audacity to say that we were the only ones causing him trouble! And what did we expect buying an apartment in a building like this? He was arrogant and unhelpful to the extreme. The restaurateur desperately tried to calm things down a little, but we continued the discussion.

"What do you want me to do?" Kyriacos asked sarcastically shrugging his scrawny shoulders, "These people they just won't pay. You want me to pay for it myself? Or maybe you want to pay the remaining amount?" Butthead sniggered some more. Lara and I had discussed it earlier and we had come to the conclusion that, if necessary, we would do exactly that. We needed the lift to work in order to sell, and we sure as hell didn't have the luxury of waiting for Kyriacos to get off his arse and sort it out. If we had to pay two thousand pounds to get a sale then so be it. It was just another cost that was part of the overall job. At least that's the way we decided to look at it. It was a complete gamble on our part since it meant using pretty much all the cash we had left. If we did, it we would need a really quick sale in order to avoid bankruptcy. But at this point we were all out of options. You can imagine Kyriacos's face when we replied, "Yes. We will cover the outstanding money." Kyriacos's and Butthead's jaws dropped in disbelief and for once he had briefly lost his cool.

But this was not the end of it. Shockingly Kyriacos said no! We couldn't believe it. We had given him a no lose option, which ensured that the lift would be back up and running immediately and he said no. Had we misheard him? Had something got lost in translation? We reiterated our solution to him, but to our complete disbelief ,he was unwilling to take this option. His reasons were that everyone must pay, and until they do the lift must remain off. In the end, only after we said we would go to the lift company directly, did he agree.

The next day we paid the money and the lift was back on but we had lost one month, two thousand pounds and a load of hairs from the stress. At this point our stress in England faded into insignificance in comparison. When the lift opened it smelt so bad that we both had to wear masks. Some nice soul had decided to piss in it just before it had been turned off, and it had been sitting inside festering for the whole month. It pretty much summed the place up. But, like good little elves, we cleaned it out and considered ourselves lucky to have had the money to snatch back control from Kyriacos's greasy hands. Without delay, we contacted every Estate Agent there was. Lara had also created an amazing web site with outstanding pictures of all the apartment and views with which to advertise it!!! We were all set. Now all that was left to do was pray! Pray for a quick sale ☺.

CHAPTER 14

Contracts At Dawn

Out of the blue and still with our unresolved issues regarding parking and fees pending, we had a mail through from Pablos. In it he stated that after further searching, it appeared that our Titanic apartment did actually have an allocated parking space. Now as good news as this was it raised yet more serious questions about his competence as a lawyer. First of all this was completely contrary to what he had told us initially. It was an error, if correct, an error that could have seriously cost us money since we were selling it without parking. The difference is not only in the extra cash, that having allocated parking can bring but in the saleability. Obviously, something coming with allocated parking is much more sellable. The other issue is how, at this stage, could we possibly trust anything he was telling us. After all of his discrepancies so far and after, he himself, telling us that we didn't have allocated parking. How could we be sure he was correct this time? If he wasn't and we went ahead selling it as if it did have parking it could look even worse. And last of all, who told him to do any more searches on this matter anyway? It certainly wasn't us, as we had accepted the fact that it didn't come with parking a long time ago. We thought we needed some independent advice first of all, before finally arranging a meeting to sort all of this mess out, face to face with the man himself!

In the office of Martina, we handed our contract of sale over and she had a good look at it for us. She brought up two very good points. Firstly, the contract of sale that we ourselves had signed had no mention of the allocated parking space- obviously, as at that time we were told that there was not one. In short, this meant that even if Pablos had made a mistake and there was actually parking with this property, we would not legally own it because all we signed for was the apartment. It would, in actual fact, still be owned by the Arab! That in itself could only be considered as gross incompetence on Pablos's part, the consequence of which could only cost us money. The second point they made was that the title deeds could be easily misread by an inexperienced lawyer. It did mention parking, but when you look a bit closer, on the next page it gives the plot numbers who own the space, of which ours was not one. The outcome was that we definitely did not have an allocated parking space. Also regarding the Kapparis situation they advised us that we most definitely should have received plans to show which parking space was ours. Only on older buildings did they not have plans for the parking areas and this was not one of them. We needed a meeting with Pablos A.S.A.P to sort this, the Kapparis parking issue and the discrepancy with his figures out.

Pablos's office hadn't changed one iota since our last visit. If anything it had got worse! The files were piled higher and the papers were scattered further. Still no computer in sight either! It was no wonder he made so many mistakes. In such a clutter it was amazing he didn't lose his own mind! We all sat around his large meeting desk, and pulled out our contracts and relevant papers like guns. It was like a scene from a spaghetti western and we were Clint!

It soon became very clear that it was Maria who really new about our cases. Despite this, Pablos continued to talk as if he was the one in control. Surprisingly, there was no contention regarding his figures and fees discrepancies. Lara had spent the whole of the previous evening trawling through all our money transfers and fees charged, documenting every one of them and every one of his discrepancies. It had been a real feat, as it had become a real web of mails and transfers that had by now stretched over months, but after painstakingly doing this, she had compiled all of the listed discrepancies and proof of transfers etc in one big mail for them to go over. Any lawyer would have been proud of such a fantastic presentation of a case. It had clearly worked! The frightening thing is that it took all of this for them to agree that their figures were wrong. Lesser people would never have been able to do all of this, and would have just paid the extra amounts. We wondered how many people out there have done exactly that?

With a victory on the money situation under our belts, the next issue to approach was the apparent parking at our Titanic apartment. Was there parking or not? Pablos raced ahead and showed us the contract. He confidently told us that there definitely was parking allocated, as he pointed to the part on the front document. We told him we believed that there was not, and to have a look at the next page. Maria took the contract off him and had a good look at it herself. It was Maria who originally told us that there was no parking with this property. After another look at it she told us that we were correct and there was actually no parking. Pablos grabbed it back off her and took another look at the section Maria was now pointing out to him. Needless to say, he was looking rather disgruntled but did not admit to misreading the document.

We looked at each other in disbelief. Maybe we should have been charging him for our legal advice? His vague excuse, I quote him now was "you know how it is…sometimes you just answer things off the top of your head." Just the sort of lawyer you really need! I think I'd rather represent myself! So with another victory, shallow as it was, on the Titanic parking front in the bag, we moved onto Kapparis and the situation regarding parking there.

Maria pulled this folder out from the bottom of her files and extracted the relevant contracts. As it sat there on the table in front of us we could not believe our eyes. It was a plan. A plan of all the allocated parking spaces. All clearly numbered. The very plan that Pablos had told us did not come with this property. The same one that he said would cost us extra money to do a deeper search at the land registry to obtain. The very one that we had been requesting for all of this time! We picked it up and with it, it was as clear as daylight exactly where our parking space was. Well of course it was, I mean, it was a plan after all and generally that's what plans do!!! We both looked in disbelief at Pablos, and asked him why we had not received this? The response we received from Maria was, "Oh, didn't you get this?"

"No!" we both screamed. "You told us the plan did not come with the deeds and that you would need to do a special search at further expense to us to get it. You even told us that this building was too old to have plans."

"Oh! I'll run you off a copy now then," Maria replied, cool as a cucumber while Pablos sat there smiling like a baboon. I'm glad he was happy because we sure as hell weren't! Never at any point, for anyone of the above issues, did we receive so much as an apology for their clear counts of incompetence or if you want to be polite, mistakes. If it was on just one transaction, maybe you could pass it off as a mistake. I mean, everyone's human and what with the added language factor things can always get lost in translation, especially via email and over the phone. But these were errors on three completely separate cases and we know for a fact, that the same things were happening with a friend of ours, who also purchased a studio and had them dealing with it. He was getting the same discrepancies with the figures and fees.

Really, I think incompetence is being polite. I think some might say incompetence and dishonesty!

We left Pablos's office feeling a sense of relief and disbelief! Relief in that we had finally cleared these few loose ends up but also complete and utter disbelief at their complete and utter incompetence. Needless to say we would not be using them in the future. However, unbeknown to us our paths would be forced to cross for one last time!

CHAPTER 15

The Price of Fish

When it comes to valuations Cyprus is no different to England. Estate Agents valuations are as variable as exchange rates! Finally, it was that time. The moment of truth that all renovators dread, when they finally get to discover whether all their predictions of value are correct, or just shattered dreams. The dreaded valuation! All of the invites had been sent out now it was time to sit back and let the games begin.

Unlike Noah's animals, the Estate Agents marched in one by one in order to give their "expert" opinions on the price of our property. At this stage of the game, we desperately needed positivity and, like a miracle it, came to us in the heavenly form of...Jed!!! He waltzed in with a glow on his face, as if he had just clenched some more sales, or perhaps he was thinking about all the commission he was likely to make on this one? As he entered, he was clearly taken back by the transformation that stared him straight in the eye. He was lost for words which for an Estate Agent is pretty much unheard of.

"The building doesn't seem quite as bad as I remember it," he remarked, "and the lift's O.K then?" He seemed completely surprised. Little did he know that it had been us who had single-handedly repaired and painted all of the corridors, reception area and lift. It had been us who had paid out of our own pockets to get the lift up and running again. And why he was surprised that the lift was working was very curious! After all, it was working when he showed to us. The only reason we could think of was that he knew damned well the trouble they had had with it previously. But we stood, smiled and said nothing other than that the committee had finally got together, and were gradually getting the works done. Yeah right! We were feeding him the same sort of crap that he would have fed us. He was, of course, visually surprised for some unknown reason! We don't know why, after all he was the one who said what a great buy this apartment was! He wondered around in complete wonderment at the transformation we had achieved. Despite all of his advice and profit projections when he sold us this place, he obviously never really believed that we could really turn it around. In fairness, he never really knew us.

After he had taken a good look, we all sat down at the table and began to tackle that most important question of all. How much is it worth? Baring in mind we had asked Jed this question a few months earlier, before we had finished and before he had seen it. At that time, he told us, as he did when he sold it to us, that it would be worth about £95k CYP. We were really hoping for more than that! As he sat, I could see him reaching up to his pie in the sky and grabbing off a chunk. He pulled it down and presented it to us. His new improved figure was... £150k CYP. Needless to say we were gob smacked! But great as this figure was it was a world away from his previous estimation and to be honest it sounded a bit far fetched. However, we prayed he was right because at that price we'd have made a huge profit. Happy days! But we were very keen to be realistic with our price. Not to over price it and have it festering on the market for months. We needed to get a quick sale. At least Jed left us with the positive news that we so desperately needed. But after all, that was what Jed was the master at. Telling people what they wanted to hear, and exactly when they want to hear it!

A few more expat agents followed, and all of them were overwhelmed with the job we had done on the apartment, and with the apartment itself. All of them loved the views and the décor. We even had one of them suggesting that we do this for other people- design and renovate for the specific purpose of making properties more saleable. He actually had someone in mind who would have gladly paid us for our services. This was obviously a real complement, but we declined the offer as we were out here to do our own projects, and judging by this one they would be taking up enough of our time.

The other common comment that kept on being used was, I quote, "Great apartment, shame about the building!" It became a private game we played to guess how long it would be before they made this comment. Usually it was just as we were sitting down discussing the price. Despite this, the common consensus was that it was worth around £120k CYP, which was much more realistic than Jed's valuation, but still great news for us. It was the price we had thought it would be worth and at that price, if we could obtain it, we would have made a respectable profit. These agents were all really excited about listing it and thought we'd have no problems selling. I know what you're thinking, that all agents tell you that. Well whilst in England you are probably correct, out here as we discovered, the Cypriot agents don't!

Cue Andreas, our first local Cypriot agent who came stomping in like an unimpressed bull. Judging from the distressed look on his face he had clearly made up his mind before he had even entered into the apartment. He raced around the entire apartment in a few seconds flat, barely even glimpsing at the view. And as he did so he made the sarcastic comment, "Huh. After a month you won't even see it!" At the door on his way out he continued his appraisal, "Just as I expected. Whilst the apartment looks great the real issue here is the building (*as if we didn't know that already!*). Unfortunately, it's not a complete package and as a result will be almost impossible for me to sell! This building is one of the worst! As far as a price is concerned," he paused for a second deep in thought, caressing his rather large stubbly chin as he pondered over the question, "well really I couldn't even give you a price on it. It has no price! But obviously I can't turn down your listing. So let me know the price you want to list it for."

With those words of wisdom he left us, and like a shooting star in the midnight sky that was the last we ever saw of him. Thank god! In deed he left us both deeply confused and pondering over his riddle. I mean, what on earth had he meant? Lara, who always looks at the glass as half full, thought that he had meant that because the apartment was so unique, like art it was very difficult to put a price on. And would in fact be worth whatever someone might wish to pay for it. E.g. someone might fall in love with it and be willing to pay a fortune for it. Well I on the other hand, am more of a realist, though some might say pessimist, and judging from the distressed look on his face when he entered, and the frown on his face as he left, believed him to mean that it was not worth anything unless we were extremely lucky. Lucky enough to get someone interested who loved what we had done with it, and was prepared to overlook the state of the actual building! Either way we were guessing and his visit did not help us one iota!

The only thing we were thankful for was that Andreas wasn't our first agent. I think at that stage, if he was, we would probably have slit our wrists and committed a joint suicide. However, Andreas's opinion seemed to be the common consensuses amongst the Cypriot agents. Completely contradictory to the English ones. It seemed that the local Cypriot agents were completely biased against these types of buildings. In fairness, they probably knew better than anybody else the realities of actually living in them. What, with the years of neglect, problems with common expense money collection, the type of residents living in them, and lets not forget the earthquake factor. With all this in mind, they had already made up their minds before ever even entering the apartment. Also, with some of them, I think they don't like to see foreigners coming out and making money. Either way their valuations were all considerably lower at around the 90k mark. As far as flexibility on fees was concerned, the Cypriot agents were the worst. They were about as flexible as ten inch iron pole!

Ultimately, it's always up to you what price you put your property up for. We reckon usually, taking into consideration all of your valuations, the correct value is somewhere in the middle plus a bit extra to allow for the usual bartering. Most buyers like to feel they've managed to knock the price down a bit. I suppose you could call this one the feel good factor. With this in mind we finally decided on listing it at £125k CYP. In English terms this is a fantastic price for a huge three bedroom apartment over looking the sea. My sister is currently looking to get on the property ladder in the U.K. for the first time, and she like so many others can't even get a shoe box of a one bedroom for less than £100k GBR. And the only views they've got are of main roads! But be very wary of making the mistake of comparing one country's prices to another's. The prices are always specific to that particular country and can not be compared. Although this may sound cheap to your average English person coming over for a one week stay, this price sounds expensive to a local person who is on a lower wage etc. So be careful not to pay too much because you're thinking in English terms! Unless that is, you happen to be buying one of our properties. Then please feel free to pay as much as you want ☺

With our price now set we wasted no time in informing all the relevant agents. The good thing to remember out here with the Estate Agents, is that although they may charge extortionately high commissions, you do not have to go sole agent. In fact, our advice is to get listed with as many as you possibly can. Buy yourself a huge "for sale" sign, and stick it up outside your property with your own number on it too. You never know, you might just get lucky and someone will call you direct, thus avoiding those huge Estate Agents fees. Stick adds in the local papers too. Do anything and everything possible to sell your property. Don't just rely on any one agent.

Though our property was now listed with just about every Estate Agent on the island, our predicament had not changed. We still needed a sale and we needed it quickly. In short we needed a miracle if we were going to stay afloat and in Cyprus.

CHAPTER 16

A Committee Nightmare

Becoming a committee member had proved to be a complete nightmare. Soon after the honey moon period was over we began getting calls from one of the resident owners called Paniotis. He was one of the previous committee members and was the only one who lived in the actual block. A strange little man, in his mid forties. A funny smell always surrounded him, and his dark chest hair was always on parade for everyone to see, like it or not! However, he began to ring us just about every day with the silliest of reasons. Reasons such as, "could you help clear all of the rubbish in the garden?... where are the rubbish sacks?... Where can we burn it all?... How do you start a fire?" (... *with a match!*) "We must have CCTV installed... We must have sprinklers installed and a private grassed area created with lounges... We mast have a door entry system installed and new letter boxes... Meet Mrs Alidopilas who lives on the 3rd floor. She really needs the lift to work as she has very bad knees and it keeps breaking down... When will all the works get done..? How far have you got with them?.."

The list went on and on. All things that he himself had done nothing about for all those years! He hassled us so much that in the end we had to change our phone number. We were sure he was doing this in an attempt to show us how difficult it was to be a committee member. Some vain attempt to try and make himself not feel so useless for all the years he sat back and did nothing. Despite him, we struggled on but as hard as we tried it soon became very clear that we were never going to be able to collect all of the common expense money in without either the help of the Krays or the courts. Now since the Krays were not only not in Cyprus, but were now dead, the courts seemed our only option. Though I still believed we probably stood more chance of getting the money with the dead Krays than through the courts, but I suppose only time would tell.

It was the same people, most of whom were the old committee members who just refused to pay anything. Most of them saying they wouldn't pay anything unless they knew the others were paying. None of them wanting to be the ones who were paying when others weren't. Just a convenient excuse! With this type of mentality to deal with, it didn't take a genius to see we were going to get nowhere, and fast, without legal assistance. Also it raised the question that if it was proving to be this difficult to get the smallest amounts out of these idiots, how on earth were we ever going to get the large amount that we would need from them for the main building works? Who knows! The one thing we did know was that it was time to get some legal advice to determine the way forward.

We set a meeting with our "good" solicitor, Martina who had dealt with cases like this in the past. The advice she gave us was that we should get our quotes in first of all. Then present the chosen one to the owners and give them a month to pay the required amount. After this, we would need to proceed down the legal route. Not just for these funds but also to force them to pay the common expenses. It all sounded good. Now we had a clear path to follow with a solicitor in place. So our first step was to get the quotations in. Easy you might think. Well you'd be wrong. I mean, this is Cyprus after all and there are only two things that come easy out here, getting a tan and getting a headache!

As required we approached a number of contractors hoping to obtain our three quotes. We began this process in July but due to the August break here, we couldn't even get anyone out to have a look until September. When they did come out to look the reactions were not good. In the end there was only one contractor who was willing to do the works his name was Andreas. The others wouldn't even touch it, saying that it was in such a bad state that it really needed to be pulled down. Unfortunately, pulling it down was not an option. Our contractor, Andreas, proposed reinforcing the columns and went off to prepare his quotation. It was only after numerous calls to chase him up for his elusive quotation that we finally received it a whole month later in October. It was approximately sixty thousand pounds giving Demis a near coronary failure. I think he only expected the cost of repairs to amount to about twenty thousand. Needless to say Demis wasn't a happy chappy! He was determined to get this quote reduced, so he immediately put it back to Andreas and asked him to come up with a better quote for us. In a way this was a good thing since petty much everything is open to a bit of bartering in Cyprus- from buying a TV to purchasing a pair of spectacles. It's always worth trying to barter the price down, and most shops already allow for it in their prices.

The only trouble was that in doing so it wasn't until January 2006 that Andreas, finally, after much chasing and Christmas breaks etc, gave us his new improved quotation. Sure enough it was ten thousand pounds cheaper but it had taken approximately four more months. This new quote was now fifty thousand pounds and once split between nineteen apartments it worked out at about two and a half thousand pounds each. In return, we would all end up with a fantastic looking apartment block and grounds. The value of each of our apartments would have shot up to about ninety thousand pounds each. Not bad heh? Now bearing in mind most of these guys had purchased their apartments for about twenty thousand pounds, this wasn't a bad return for their investment! With that in mind, you would have expected there to have been no problem getting the said payment off the owners. No need for solicitors. No need for stress. It's only logical after all, but as we have started to realise, logic dose not reside in Cyprus! Anyway the letters went out and all that was left to do was sit back and wait for a month to see if legal action was going to be really necessary.

Meanwhile, back at Titanic, we were still at high alert and assigned to our vigilante duties. With the property now listed it was even more important to keep it, and all the common areas leading to it, looking good. This was to be an ongoing mission against hidden rebel forces using guerrilla tactics. Most people think it's the building works that are the big headache. In our case the actual building works were the least of our problems. Trying to maintain this building in order to sell was proving to be one of our biggest and bloodiest of battles ever. From the constant dumping to the endless graffiti, trying to maintain our white paint and roof areas took real determination and unprecedented persistence. We had become resident unpaid caretakers of Titanic- to the annoyance of the teenagers.

When finally the rains came for the first time since we had arrived, it soon became clear that the roof was going to be a real issue. With every downpour, entire lakes were created. When the roofers re-laid the new roof, they conveniently forget about a little thing called drainage. The water also pooled up above the outer hall corridor section. This section of roof was completely shot, so any water here just soaked right through, and would drip down onto the hallway outside our apartment if unattended too. We had just had that section in the hallway re-plastered so we had to do something about this problem, other-wise the plaster would have soon been ruined in that area.

So, in the wake of the storm, we were up there with our mops. Mopping the water off the roof. The funny thing was that when we looked out across all the other roof tops we could see many others like ourselves on top of their roofs mopping and sweeping too. We were not alone! Their roofs had large lakes too. Beware of Cyprus roofs. As I said before, they are notori-ously bad and the frightening thing is that if you buy your prop-erty in the summer months you'll never know! Look out for the tell tail damp patches on the ceilings, or that out of place fresh coat of paint! Believe you me they don't paint unless absolutely necessary! As fate would have it, from then on, the rains began to fall almost every day. And every time we were forced to go topside.

They say that human ingenious is amazing, and we too devised some cunning tricks to make the water shifting easier. If ever you're in a similar position to us, which you probably will be if you buy a top floor apartment in Cyprus, we would advise you to purchase the following items:

1 long length of plastic tubing,
1 dustpan, brush not necessary,
1 big bucket
1 mop and squeezer bucket.

You're probably wondering what the heck all of this is for? Well listen close. The length of plastic piping is used to siphon off the worst of the water. The dust pan, forget the brush, is used to scoop the water up and then with the dustpan full, empty into the bucket. I know it sounds stupid but it works. To finish the job use the mop. As completely demoralising as this was, since no sooner than we had finished the rain tended to come again just to spite us, it was not the worst of our problems.

The worst of our problems were the teenagers, who began to congregate in numbers at the top of the stairwell every night. Because we were on the top floor their talking and laughter rattled right through into the apartment, as if they were inside with us. As if that wasn't bad enough they began to graffiti up in the stairwell, just outside our hallway. It began as a few scribbles, so we approached them nicely to ask them to move on and to stop graffitiing. There were two boys about seventeen years old and 6ft tall, and two girls. We were greeted with the usual sarcasm and denial that you would have expected. From their defiant looks and rude sniggers it was obviously them doing it all. What began as a few scribbles, turned into an all out graffiti fest. Within a day or two, the whole wall had suddenly become filled with the crap that only young teenage wannabe rebels could think of. Most of which was filth and rapidly spreading like wildfire down to our hallway. Now they were really taking the piss! If a potential viewer had seen it there would be no way they would buy the apartment. So with one hundred and twenty-five thousand pounds at stake we needed to do something about it and fast. Our dilemma was, what? What was the best way to handle teenage kids? Go in all guns a blazing or with cotton wool gloves on? Either way could severely back fire on us. You know what kids are like. They could storm off and maliciously graffiti or vandalise everything just to spite you.

Unfortunately, we didn't have the luxury of doing nothing and we had already tried the nice approach with no success, so we opted for the "scare the shit out of them" approach. We were going to come down on them like a tone of bricks and hope that scaring the living crap out of them would do the trick! Our plan was to watch a couple of classic pre-recorded episodes of East

Enders, the ones with Phil Mitchell doing his stuff and then the entire Krays film all in a row. After which, we should be sufficiently hyped up enough to be bad mother f****ers not to be messed with, and to be taken extremely seriously!!! You know what they say, "extreme circumstances call for extreme measures."

Needless to say, the young punks never knew what had hit them! We pounced with the subtlety of a Panzer division and caught them red handed. Literally! They were scribbling on the walls with their red marker pens. This time there could be no denial. We went in hard like two crazed maniacs. The screams and yells could be heard all the way down to the ground floor. We snatched the pens off them, and furiously threw them straight out of the window. We threatened to chuck them out of the window, together with the pens, and I think they actually believed us, so much so that they agreed to come back the next day and paint over all of their graffiti. I know what you're thinking, that they never came back the next day. Well, amazingly enough, they did.

We decided that instead of painting over it all, we'd have them sand it all off first and then paint. Needless to say, as they were sanding, their new designer clothes were getting completely covered in filth. It was all we could do to stop ourselves from cracking up as we watched them getting covered. But we had to maintain our tough exterior, otherwise they'd have seen right through us and downed tools immediately.

So, instead, we'd walk down to our apartment and only once inside, and out of sight from prying eyes, would we burst out into hysterical fits of laughter. Then we'd regain our composure and march back up again to check that the work was being done.

As funny as it seems now, this really was no joke. We had a

lot at stake and were growing very weary of the endless crap we were being forced to clear up. It certainly wasn't what we had signed up for, to become glorified unpaid caretakers to a decrepit old building that it's own residents didn't give a stuff about. And, if we had wanted to discipline rebellious teenagers, we'd have become teachers! Try as we might, we couldn't recall any of this being in Jed's sales pitch, and it sure as heck wasn't the stress free life and new beginning we had both dreamed of. One thing was for damned sure, this was no dream! This was a bloody nightmare of which we could see no end too. Freddy Krueger eat your heart out. If you really want horror come to Cyprus! At least that's the way we felt at the time. That Cypriot Estate Agent was right. View? What view???!

CHAPTER 17

Sale of the Century Part One

A few viewers, and just one week later, our prayers were answered in the form of a Czech businessman introduced to us through an Estate Agent called Alexia. If before I was a sceptic, now I truly believe in miracles, for a better buyer there could not have been. He had been back and forth from Cyprus on business for years and was fed up with hotel rooms. He was a cash buyer and wanted to complete the sale A.S.A.P, which for obvious reasons couldn't be quick enough for us! As if that wasn't amazing enough, he offered us one hundred and eighteen thousand pounds which we duly accepted. This was just too good to be true. We couldn't help but wonder whether this was just another part of the sick twisted game that we felt god was playing with us, and that at any minute he would just whisk the Czech back up to heaven on a cloud. Well, amazingly enough, this buyer was for real. There was of course just one catch... All of this had been arranged via his P.A. She had been set the remit by him to find him a nice sea view apartment. It had been her who had been to see the apartment. He had to view it for himself before the deal was confirmed, and he was back in a week's time.

That week was the longest week of our lives. The heavens decided to open at least twice, and some arsehole decided to dump the smeggiest flowery off-green sofa you have ever smelt right out side the main entrance door. Of course we were the ones who had to dispose of it. But true to his word, on Monday morning at about eleven o'clock, the Czech came. Everything was looking great, but then again the pixies had been at it since eight, touching up, cleaning and mopping. The lift was looking clean, and with the aid of some air freshener, was smelling of sweet summer meadows. Our movie magic was holding up perfectly. For once, things seemed to be going in our favour. It was a glorious day and the view was looking absolutely magnificent. It seemed as if finally luck was on our side. Our one concern was that he might be over six foot tall. You see as great as our power shower was, a slight error had been made in the erection of it. Whilst it was absolutely divine to use, it was not, shall we say, designed for the vertically advanced. It was perfect for us but we were both under six foot tall. Anybody over might have had a slight problem.

When the knock on the door came we jumped like excited school kids trying desperately not to look too desperate. If he got so much as a whiff of our desperation we could kiss good buy to any hopes of getting a high price. We opened the door tentatively to reveal the shortest short-arse Czech businessman there has ever been. "Yes!" we both screamed out to each other telepathically. Things just could not have been any better! Praise the lord! Hallelujah. It was as if subconsciously we had designed this entire apartment just for him!

The viewing went without a hitch. He loved it. Now it was just a case of sorting out the paperwork. There was just one thing he was absolutely insistent on. He would only complete with the named owners. In short that meant the people whose names were on the title deeds. In our case, it was not us, so this presented yet another problem. It was still the Arab's name on the title deeds. There was nothing dodgy about this it just generally takes time for the title deeds to get transferred into non-Cyprus resident's names. Of course all the contracts of sale had been signed between the Arab and us and so we did legally own it.

The added problem we had was the flat we were living in, had just been approved by the council of ministers for the title deeds to be transferred into our names. The problem with this, was that non-residents could only have one property registered in their name. Whilst this was a problem, it also turned out to be a blessing in disguise. Thankfully, Martina had a couple of ways around this issue. Our first option, and our preferred option, was to get the Arab to cancel his contract with us and sign a new contract direct with the Czech. The upside to this was that we would avoid ever having to pay transfer fees, which would be five percent of the purchase price. The capital gains would have to be split. The Arab would have to pay his up to our purchase price, and we would pay the rest. The downside to this, was that he was in Dubai. Unless he happened to be in the country, he would have to sign power of attorney over to his solicitor to sort things out on his behalf.

Obviously this would all take time, and the Czech was an impatient man, so Alexia kept telling us. He wanted to get in as soon as possible. But we had to give it a shot since from our point of view, if we could pull it off, we stood to save over two thousand pounds. After two weeks and never ending calls from Alexia, we decided that plan A wasn't working. We couldn't risk loosing the Czech, so on to plan B. Plan B was as follows. Fortunately for us we had a letter of approval from the Council of Ministers for deeds of our home to be transferred into our names. What we could do was to cancel our contract for that, and then switch the details for Titanic. Thus getting permission for the Titanic title deeds to be transferred into our names instead. To do this, we needed to get a new contract drawn up between the original vendors of our home, and somebody other than us who we could trust not to run off with it, i.e. Lara's parents. Then, we would also need a cancellation contract between the original vendor and ourselves.

Because Lara's parents weren't in Cyprus, we would need the services of our favourite incompetent solicitor Pablos one last time. He still had P.O.A for Lara's parents from the Kapparis apartment job, hence could sign all the relevant documents on their behalf. Anna also needed the reference number off Pablos for our application to the Council of Ministers, for the title deeds to be transferred into our names for Titanic. She needed this in order to withdraw that application. I know it sounds unbelievably complicated but it could just save us our sale. And besides, it was the only plan left!

Just when we thought Pablos couldn't get any more incompetent we discovered that we were wrong! In asking him for our reference number it turned out that he had actually "forgotten" to register our Contract of Sale for Titanic altogether so no application had ever been made to the Council of Ministers for permission to transfer the title deeds, nor our Contract of Sale lodged at the land registry. Yes, that's right, he actually said that he forgot! Well, actually, he didn't say *he* forgot, he said his colleague in Limassol forgot. Of course, again we got no apology. But it was fair to say that his incompetence had shot up to a level we never knew even existed. If incompetence had a league system, Pablos would have been in the premiership! I mean, how can your solicitor forget to do something as important as that? To submit your application in for approval is the key thing you are paying them to do.

Without an application you can never be approved, and thus the title deeds will never be transferred into your name. In short, you will never be the true owner. There is also the other issue to consider. All the while your contract of sale is not submitted to the land registry office you are left in an extremely vulnerable position. You see, until this is done, the previous owner is still the registered owner and therefore could, if unscrupulous enough, resell the property to someone else. Of course this is not legal, but no one would be any the wiser until the second purchaser goes to submit their Contract of Sale, at which point it would probably be too late. This unscrupulous seller would be long gone with two lots of sales proceeds in his or hers bank account. It will be you who is left to argue the toss with the second purchaser and sort out the ensuing mess that will inevitably follow. Make no mistake, this is not just a hypo-thetical situation that has never happened. This type of incident has and does go on. The world is not full of honest honourable people!

If we hadn't have needed this reference number we would never have known. Maybe after a year we'd be wondering why we hadn't had the new title deeds. We'd have probably given him a ring, and only then would he have discovered his mistake. Then we'd have to start the process again, not that it was ever started in the first place, having to wait another six months to a year. And if he "forgot" once, then how could we ever trust him not to "forget" again? Something as insignificant as this could just slip right through his mind! Couldn't it? Well fortunately this would not be a concern for us for much longer. As it turned out, with no application ever submitted, it actually made Martina's job a lot easier. It meant that there was no application to have to bother cancelling. So perhaps we should have been thanking him? ...not!!!

Anyway, we did get Pablos to sign the relevant documents, on behalf of Lara's parents, to put our home in their names. The irony was, that he insisted on contacting them first to confirm this was O.K. Whilst this was of course the correct thing for him to do, it was, as I said, an irony for two reasons. Firstly, in this instance there was nothing for them to loose. In fact we were asking him to sign a document on their behalf to say that they would become the owners of our property in Limassol. Nothing to pay, just a fifty thousand pound property to gain. Nice one! Secondly, there was the small fact that he had never asked them to confirm anything before. Not with any of the Kapparis documents that needed signing, or any of the money transfers relating to Kapparis. Oh well, I suppose at least he was getting better!

Now to conclude our dealings with him and finally get closure, there was one last thing. We needed to get back all of the P.O.A documents. All the ones for us and Lara's parents. Now we were living in Cyprus there was no need for him to have P.O.A. I suppose this request really put his nose out of joint. It was the final nail in the coffin of what had been an extremely rocky relationship to say the least. But, he handed them over, and with documents firmly grasped in hand we flew out of his office like the wind. As we exited he shouted out to us, "See you soon." Telepathically we both replied, with strained smiles, "Not if we see you first!" We swear from the shocked look on his face that he heard us! Oh well, who cares?

The next day we handed over all of the documents to Martina. Now all that was left to do was get the previous owners of our home to sign the cancellation contract with us, and the new contract with Lara's parents. Then once Martina had all of these contracts signed they could present them to the land registry and hopefully obtain our new title deeds for Titanic in our names. Then she could start on the contract between the Czech and ourselves. Hopefully this would not take too long. Anyway, there was nothing more we could do. It was all in the very capable hands of Martina. It was time now to sit back and relax, although relaxing was something that in Titanic was for us pretty much impossible!

Another week passed and still no action. Martina had been

unable to obtain the signatures needed from the previous owners of our home. It was a very simple matter. All they needed to do was sign the cancellation contract between us, and then resign the exact same contract but in Lara's parents names. It wasn't as if they had to travel from miles away either. They were local people. They kept telling Martina that they would be in tomorrow to sign, but of course tomorrow never came. The really annoying thing was, that they had ripped us off with this property. They had told us a pack of lies regarding it and since speaking to our neighbours, we found out that they had not owned it long, and actually made a huge profit on it for doing nothing.

But after the second week came and went without any signatures from them, it was obvious that they weren't going to put themselves out on our behalf! Of course by the second week of waiting, we were receiving ever increasing amounts of annoying phone calls, texts and emails from Alexia repeating the same questions like a broken record. "What's happening? When will the deeds be transferred into your names? What's taking so long?" They became increasingly pressuring. I think she was starting to fear that her easy five percent was slipping away from her. But her constant calls etc. were not helping. Calls such as, "He says that he'll pull out unless it's all completed by the 28th. So you must have the deeds in your name by then!" That was only ten days away, and besides there was nothing more we could do push this matter along anyway. If there was we would have done it!

The worst of it was that Alexia, despite our requests for her to get some sort of deposit off him, had not done so. This left us in a really vulnerable state yet again, as by now our legal fees were mounting up. If he did pull out now we would have been royally screwed. On hindsight, we should have pushed much harder for a deposit off him. Without it, we should not have taken the property off the market, and certainly should not have started legal proceedings. But we were desperate. With our funds running out and no other offers on the table we needed this deal, and didn't want to do anything to jeopardise it. Also, being a cash buyer who wanted to complete in two weeks, we never imagined we would run into the complications we ran in to. We thought that it would all be completed in the two weeks. By the time you'd have got the deposit off him, it would have been time to pay the whole amount and barely enough time for anyone to back out. But my advice to you is, be firm and make sure you get a deposit before going any further.

Now in the fifth week our real fly in the ointment was still the previous owner who still hadn't signed anything. It suddenly became extremely clear what their true motives were, and just how greedy they were. They had sensed an opportunity to extract yet more cash out of us. The husband informed Martina that they would not sign anything, unless we agreed in writing to pay any tax above and beyond the original contract price. There were two issues with this. The first, as well they knew, was the tax is determined on a valuation of the property at the time of the transfer of the deeds. In other words, the price on the contract may not be the price they value it at, and hence not the taxable price. It could be lower or it could be higher. Obviously, in Cyprus, property prices have been rising, so it could be assumed that the value would have increased and hence the tax would also have increased. This was always their responsibility to pay, as it is of every vendor, not ours. The second issue, as well they knew, which compounded the problem was that we agreed to sign what's called a split contract.

This is a very common procedure in Cyprus. It's basically a way to reduce the amount of transfer tax the vendor will pay. A bit of a tax dodge you might say ☺ What happens is that the total purchase price is split and two contracts are drawn up. One is called the immovable property contract, this one is for the actual property itself and is taxable. The other one is called the movable property contract, this one is for the furniture etc within the property and is not taxable. The idea is to reduce, on paper, the price of the actual property. This in turn, reduces the amount of tax to be paid upon transfer. For instance, in this case, the property was really sold for fifty-two thousand pounds which would have brought it into the five percent tax bracket. A split contract brought the property price under fifty thousand and hence put it into the three percent tax bracket. Also, it would appear that less total profit had been made, and so would reduce the total amount of capital gains tax required to pay. Now at twenty percent of profit that can amount to quite a substantial amount.

Well, whilst this was fantastic for them, it now presented a problem for us. If we signed the agreement to pay the additional tax, due to the fact that on paper, it appeared that we purchased the apartment for far less than we really did. It would appear, when valued at the current market value by the tax department, that we had made a huge profit. In turn, the likelihood of us having to pay yet more tax was extremely high! But in truth they had us by the short and curlies and they knew it! What could we do? Agree to their terms or lose a huge sale? It's amazing how all these little unforeseen costs can really start to eat away at your profit like cancer!!!

Reluctantly, we signed a separate agreement between us as they wanted, which meant Martina could now get our application changed at the Council of Ministers for that of Titanic. Given the speed that things happen out here, it was highly unlikely that we'd have the title deeds in our names by Monday 28th which was when the Czech wanted, but at least he would be able to see that it was all under way. A letter from the Council of Ministers saying we had approval for the title deeds to be transferred to our names, meant that we would soon be the legal owners, and that the title deeds would be following shortly and just a formality. With that obtained, he could confidently sign the Contract of Sale with us and thus complete on the deal. From his point of view, once signed and the money was handed over to us, he could move in almost immediately and take full possession of Titanic in all it's magnificence! Needless to say, it couldn't be quick enough for us, but with things going the way they had been, we weren't counting our chickens quite yet. I mean, a lot could happen over a weekend and as they say, "it ain't over till the fat lady sings!" And in our case, she sure as hell wasn't getting out of bed for nothing. Her fees had gone up. Now she wanted nothing less than blood and guts!

Now at this point it's Saturday morning November 26th 2005 and as you can see I've kind of caught up with myself. I'm sitting here on the white leather corner sofa in our lovely penthouse apartment, Titanic, looking out across the room to the deepest blue most tranquil sea I have ever seen. The ocean's as still as a pond and the sun is sparkling across the few ripples there like divine diamonds. The apartment is filled from top to bottom with that glorious fresh leather smell that only ever comes from newly born leather sofas. Sofas, that haven't lost their zest through the vigour's of endless butts being perched upon them. Coast FM's radiating out from the kitchen radio telling me that this is "as good as it gets." Well maybe it is. Maybe this is as good as it gets. This is after all why we came out here. To be able to eat breakfast with stunning views like the one right in front of me, and to have the awe-inspiring ocean just a stones throw away. I'm thinking that if all goes well on Monday despite everything we might actually miss this place. We'll miss the luxury that we've created inside this apartment and the sanctuary away from reality that it holds within.

But suddenly a yell reverberates up from one of the other apartments below, and then the clang of the lift motor starting up above rattles abruptly through the apartment, and my daydream is shattered and I am dragged firmly back to reality. I am suddenly all too aware that I only need to step outside the front door to remind myself exactly why we must sell. With that in mind, I'm now crossing my fingers and praying once again that all goes well. On Monday we might finally have the happy ending that we so desperately need. And if you're still reading this I suspect you probably need a happy ending as much as we do. Lara's on at me to just write the happy ending in now. She says that if I write it, it will happen. But I can't do that. We've come this far with the truth warts and all and I just feel I've got to see this thing right through to the end. So no make believe happy endings. This one's going to be for real! Well only today and tomorrow to go, and then I can let you all know either way. So hold on to your britches, sit back and enjoy the ride! Speak to you all then ☺

On Sunday we decided to play a game of Monopoly to pass the time. An appropriate game for us given our situation! It's amazing just how true to life Monopoly really is. How just when things are going along fine and you think you've got all you're bases covered life deals you a chance card that in the blink of an eye changes everything. You know the sort I'm talking about. For instance, you've just gone out on a limb and spent your last pound on hotels for your properties. Now all you've got to do is sit back, and wait for your opponent to throw unlucky, and land on one for you to get all your cash back with interest. The only trouble is, instead of them throwing unlucky, you do. You land on chance, pick up the card and then there it is staring you in the face like the grim reaper. Your worst nightmare of a card. You must pay property tax on all of your hotels. Suddenly, the pressures back on and the game is a foot once again. Well, the week that followed was full of more thrills and spills than any game of Monopoly could ever offer. It was Monday the 28th and we had still not had any word back from the Council of Ministers regarding our all important approval for the title deeds to be transferred into our names. Things were tense enough as they were, when, out of the blue, we received our dreaded chance card in the form of an email from the Czech.

From: The Czech
Sent: 28 November 2005 08:13
To: Pete & Lara
Subject: Flat Sale

Dear Lara and Pete,

It is near one month since our meeting and agreeing on a sale.

To my surprise you do not have documents in order regarding this which I find surprising. It is not my business though. I like the flat and hoped for a quick settlement like we agreed.

You have assured me I should count on you and I have now been patient for one month, yet still I do not have good news except encouraging messages from Alexia.

I make plans today for my travel and shall be in Limassol on Monday, December 2005. Not for long though – only to settle the flat for look to rent.

You should check with your lawyer as you may need a permit (local formality) to owe flat in Cyprus since it was bought before Cyprus joined the EU – this may delay things.

(*** We only purchased the property in March and Cyprus joined the EU the previous year! And what exactly does he think we have been doing for the past month!!! – He could not have spoken to his solicitor or Alexia as they both are being kept up to date! ***)

I feel my position is exposed and being open, if you can complete in a week tell me at your earliest convenience. From December 5, 2005 onwards, you would need to look for another buyer. Simply, I don't have any more to wait.

Best wishes,
The Czech

∞

This was precisely the reason why it is so important to obtain a reservation deposit off your buyer. At least then you have some money in from them to cover any legal fees incurred if they decide, for no good reason, to pull out of the sale. In not doing so, we had left ourselves in another vulnerable position. We had been running around like maniacs trying to move everything along and were now going to incur far more costs than we otherwise would have had to. Not to mention taking our "For Sale" sign down and the apartment off the market for him which would have lost us yet more potential sales opportunities. We had done all of this on good faith, which clearly is not worth the paper it's written on. For him to pull out at this stage would have been devastating. Of course, no skin off his nose since he hadn't put down any reservation fee. As far as we were concerned his mail was a damned cheek.

To say he was loosing his patience after only a month, and to tell us that after next Monday we must find ourselves another buyer after being so near to doing everything he wanted was just wrong. However, he was our only offer and so clearly had the upper hand, and knew it. With this final deadline presented to us on a Czechoslovakian platter, and with no other offers on the table, the pressure was right back on us. We desperately needed to get the approval rushed through if we were going to stand any chance of meeting his deadline. If not, we could kiss this sale goodbye. It was time to bring out our secret weapon!!!

We were told Martina's woman in the land registry office had a weakness for milk chocolates. So the next day, we dropped her off a box for all her hard work in trying to push our application through, hint, hint ☺. It seemed to do the trick because by Wednesday we had our approval confirmed, and raced over to collect the letter which was as good as proof as anybody could possibly require, short of the actual title deeds ,that they were in the process of being transferred into our names. In fact, it would take about one month from approval before actually receiving the new title deeds, but with this letter as proof contracts could be drawn up and signed in advance. In this way we could meet the Czech's deadline, as long as he accepted it, which knowing this guy was not taken as said. But it was the best we could do. All that was left to make the new transfer of names legitimate, was to go down to the Land Registry office with the previous owner or his representative, i.e. his solicitor with P.O.A in this matter, and get them to sign the deeds over to us and to pay any outstanding taxes. We were also going to be required to pay the transfer fee.

As usual there was yet one more problem. On contacting the Arab's solicitor, Martina discovered that he was away until Monday. Shit!!! In one fail swoop our chances of meeting the Czech's deadline had been slashed. The chances of getting the

Arab's solicitor to come down with us to the Land Registry on the day of his return were even slimmer. Things were not looking good! We were so near and yet so far. Our game had dealt us not one but two crap cards in a row. Now at this stage in a real game of Monopoly you would expect our run of bad luck to be over. I mean, after all there are a few good chance cards as well.

On Thursday there was still no change, and it appeared we were destined to miss our deadline and lose our sale. After all the headaches and hard work we had put in to meet the Czech's demands we were stumped by the absence of the Arab's solicitor. We had put up a good fight but it appeared that we were destined to fall at the last hurdle. As you can imagine, at this stage we were feeling down and out beyond belief. We were surely on the last legs of our game, when only bankruptcy can follow. Game over. Hasta la vista baby!!! But as you know, just like Monopoly, in the throw of the dice everything can change and things can turn around just as quickly as they began...

CHAPTER 18

The Phantom Estate Agent!!!

We had heard many mysterious stories about the illusive Phantom Estate Agent, but we were convinced he was a character formed more of fiction than fact. How wrong we were! It was Thursday early evening when we threw our double six and landed on chance once more. This time our luck was about to change for the better, or so we thought! Completely out of the blue, we had a call on our mobile from an Estate Agent called Anthony. It was rather strange as we had taken the apartment off the market since we had accepted the Czech's offer and besides, we had never even contacted an Anthony.

He told us that he had heard about our apartment through the grapevine. Apparently, the word had got around how fantastic it was and what a great job we had done. He wanted to know whether it had been sold yet, because he had a client fresh in from England who was looking for something modern and ready to move into with sea views. He had been struggling to find anything for this guy, as there seemed to be nothing with those specifications around. Better still, the guy was another cash buyer and if he liked it, could move immediately. Now I know what you're thinking, that this must be fiction! Well I shit you not, this was the god's honest truth. Of course with no deposit and the threat of our Czech buyer pulling out we agreed for this new guy to take a look. Anthony wanted to check it out for himself first of all to make sure it was suitable. No time like the present we thought so we arranged for Anthony to come around in one hour's time. If the apartment was O.K. his client would come to view the next day.

We raced back to Titanic and made all the usual preparations, and sure enough, Anthony arrived an hour later. He was about thirty and like all Estate Agents was neatly groomed, suited and booted. He was clearly impressed with what he saw, and thought the apartment was exactly what his client was looking for. Intrigued we asked him again how he had come to hear about our apartment. Apparently he had been to value the apartment three floors below us. Unbeknown to us, they had just put their apartment up for sale too. They were asking the same price for theirs as we were for ours, but without doing anything to it inside. Anthony said it was awful. They were calling it refurbished ,but he said he couldn't tell what, if anything, they had actually refurbished. Typical we thought! They had heard how much we were selling ours for and were adamant that theirs was worth the same, neither caring nor appreciating why ours was worth so much. The joke was that it was they who had told Anthony about us. A bit stupid really when you think about it! I mean, if you had the choice between a truly fully renovated, fully furnished apartment or an unfurnished, un-renovated one at the same price there would be no contest. They were potentially doing themselves out of a sale but doing us a real favour.

So this was good for us. By theirs being up for the same price as ours makes people feel like they've got a real bargain with ours. It was a slightly annoying however, as they were clearly trying to cash in on all our hard work without giving us anything towards all the painting of the common areas, which we alone had done, and more importantly, paying out of our own pocket for the lift to be fixed that they were merrily using. Curious, later we took a sneak peek at theirs, through the keyhole so to speak, and sure enough from what we could see it did indeed look awful. Inside, they had painted it a luminous anti-climb green colour. Nice! Outside in the hallway and stairwell they had done nothing. The walls looked tired and worn out, and were sprinkled all over with graffiti. Graffiti that clearly dated back years judging by the hieroglyphics. These people really didn't have a clue!

The trouble is however that this happens a lot. The people hear of someone else getting a certain price for a property, then without understanding why, greed and stupidity immediately kick in, and they then want the same for their run down old heaps. There is no reasoning and they are determined that, that price, is what they want! The real problem is this very nature makes it increasingly difficult to find properties at the right price to make it worth while putting the time and the effort into renovating them. What then happens is one of two things, they either come to their senses and after a year of not being able to sell they lower their prices (but common sense does not prevail here very often!), or people like us are forced to pay more, and as a result forced to sell for more in order to make profit. This has the knock on effect of escalating property prices, which is ironical really since it's the very thing that the Cypriots also complain about, blaming us foreign investors for their rocketing property prices!!! Anyway enough of my moan and back to the story!

Anthony went on to tell us that this whole area was in the process of being regenerated. I had heard talk of the Cyprus Prime Minister wanting to attract a more affluent clientele to Limassol in an attempt to move away from the cheaper package holiday market. Works for the regeneration of Limassol had already started, that much was true. They were already rebuilding the promenade and making new seafront walkways and cycle routes, but what we didn't know was that plans for a new marina in the old port, just a stones throw away from Titanic, had just been fast tracked. They were expecting this new marina to be completed in about two year's time and all the property values around the area were projected to increase substantially. Apparently, these old sea front buildings are ear marked to be renovated so as to look more attractive from the front. The government was going to force these works to be done.

He left us pondering over his words like a couple of memorized morons. Questioning our decision to sell. Until suddenly sanity prevailed and we snapped ourselves out of it. We couldn't believe it and both burst out into uncontrolled fits of laughter. Each of us instinctively knowing what the other was thinking. After all we had been through? After all the stress and all the Estate Agent bullshit we had swallowed. Like two fools, yet again, we were momentarily taken in by his waffle. Believing his Estate Agent words and hanging off them as if they were gospel. It only goes to show how strong their magic really is. True his magic was strong, but alas, not strong enough! Fortunately, as I said, we soon shook off his spell and snapped out of his trance. With Anthony now satisfied that this was a suitable property for his client, and us back on track and set to sell, the viewing was arranged for three o'clock the next day.

Friday three o'clock came in a flash. I still remember Lara's words as we eagerly waited for our viewer. She said to me, if he's short he'll buy it. Well they all waltzed in bang on time. He was about thirty years old and was looking for a base in Limassol. A real east end barrow-boy turned good. A young business man who started off in the rag trade and had branched out into various other enterprises such as car exports, Mercs, of course, nightclubs and now property. He had been buying up property all over the island and was apparently loaded. He whizzed around the apartment, closely followed by his giggling blond girlfriend and then Anthony. And guess what? He was another short arse!!! "Yes!" we both thought. He was in the apartment for no longer than a few minutes. He appeared to like what he saw. In the brief exchange of cockney banter we had, he described the apartment as a real "diamond in the rough." A spot on description I thought.

True to Lara's predictions, about half an hour later we had a call in from Anthony. He wanted to know what was the lowest we would accept. We told him that our other buyer had offered £120,000 CYP. A bit of an exaggeration but that's poker for you. We told him that the only offer that would make it worth our while pulling out of the deal with the Czech, was if he offered the full asking price of £125,000 CYP. So it was left. The ball was once again in their court. To be honest we expected him to come back with another offer of about two thousand pounds above the price that we said the Czech had offered. To our astonishment, he came back not ten minutes later offering the full asking price of £125,000 CYP. We could not believe our luck. Suddenly, the tables had turned in our favour for once. He just wanted to come back for another look the next day and if he was happy he would give us £5000 CYP cash as a reservation deposit and would complete as quickly or slowly as we wanted.

It all sounded like a dream come true, and of course thanks to our Czech, all the paperwork was now in the process of being in place. This time a quick sale was definitely doable. All that was left now was to contact the Czech, and give him and Alexia the bad news. Naturally, we'd hold off until tomorrow after our new buyer had taken another peek, and had hopefully, fingers crossed, given us his five thousand pounds reservation fee. The very same reservation fee that our Czech buyer should have given us, but had refused too! Something that Alexia should have taken off him on our behalf but had refused to! Choosing instead to tell us a blatant lie, that it was not normal to get reservation fees. Hmm!!! And last but not least, after the Czech's threatening email we had no reservations about taking this new improved offer. After all, for us at this stage seven thousand pounds extra was too good an offer to refuse! In fact it seemed as if their very refusal to give us a reservation deposit, was about to backfire in their faces like a blocked bazooka. That was of course, as long as all went well the next day with the English guy. There certainly was no reason to think that it wouldn't. It was really just a formality. It just goes to show that taking a reservation fee is not only to your benefit but to the benefit of everyone, the Estate Agent and the buyer included. With it everyone knows where they stand and a firm commitment has been made. Oh well ☺

Once again, we found ourselves waiting on tender hooks for tomorrow to come!!! The only trouble was that tomorrow never came! Saturday came and went with no show from our new potential buyer. After hanging around all day with no sign of our new buyer or any word from our new best friend Anthony, we had no choice but to call him to find out what the hell was going on. Something you would have expected Anthony himself would have done, just out of professionalism alone if not out of courtesy. Our first few tries got nowhere. Just ringing and no answer and then voice mail. Only on our fourth try did we finally manage to get through to him. With no apologies offered for his clients no show, or his own lack of communication, he assured us that his client would be over tomorrow on Sunday but couldn't give us an exact time due to the fact that he was opening a club in Larnaca that night so was expecting a late one. Fine, we thought, no probs. As long as we sort it out before our deadline on Monday, it was O.K. with us. So once again, we were left dangling, slightly deflated, but still on a relative high. I mean, Anthony had said nothing to make us think that anything was up, so it appeared the deal was still on.

Sunday came and still no show from our illusive potential

second buyer, or any word from our little Phantom that was Anthony. We watched helpless as the hours swept slowly by. At five o'clock in the evening we tried to call Anthony all to no avail. It seemed that his phone was conveniently turned off. By nine it was clear that no one was going to show. Thanks to yet another Estate Agent's crap, we were experiencing a roller-coaster ride of emotions that seemed to be never ending. It was driving us crazy! On Friday we were as high as kites, but now we had plummeted down to pretty much our lowest low, praying that tomorrow would pull us back up to the top once again. Anthony seemed to lack any communication skills whatsoever. Either that, or he was just plain rude and didn't give a stuff about us. I think the truth is it was a mixture of both. Either way, he had not the decency to let us know what was going on. He was obviously perfectly happy for us to waist all of our time waiting for his supposed buyer.

With our deadline looming and no word from anyone, we were in real need of information. We needed to know what we were going to do tomorrow, and this all hinged on whether or not this illusive buyer of Anthony's was going to come through or not? Without any word from our man Anthony, information was the one thing we didn't have, putting us in a very difficult position. If the Czech was serious about his deadline, without any further information about this other buyer, we were going to have to go ahead with the deal as planned. That is, as long as everything was in place, which seemed pretty unlikely, as there had been no more news from Martina either. If nothing was ready for the Czech to sign tomorrow, we'd soon find out whether he was serious or just bluffing about his deadline. If he wasn't serious, it could just buy us the much needed extra time it appeared we needed, but it wasn't going to make the stress any easier to bare. And it sure as hell wasn't going to make it any easier to know what to tell Alexia when she rings- as you could be sure she would like clockwork first thing in the morning.

I guess we'd just have to wing it. It seemed that no matter how much we pondered over all the endless possibilities, the truth was that we had no choice but to sit back and yet again wait! It's the waiting that drives you mad!

With another sleepless night under our eyes Monday morning arose, D-Day! Nine o'clock in the morning and no calls from anyone. We really needed to speak to Anthony first of all to find out whether his potential deal was still on the cards or not. True to form, he wasn't answering his phone. No surprise there! At least no call from Alexia, yet! That was one good thing. In fact no calls from anyone, not even Martina. Ten o'clock and Anthony still wasn't answering his phone, now things were becoming critical. At eleven o'clock, with no news from anybody, we decided to ring Martina. If our deadline stood any chance of being met, she would have had to have drawn up some contracts for us to sign. To our shock Martina was not there! Apparently, she hadn't been in since Thursday. Things were suddenly looking ten times worse. No solicitor meant no contracts which meant no deal! That is of course if the Czech's deadline was for real. I left a message for her and we went back to our waiting game.

The first to finally call was Martina. Thankfully, she had got the message that we had called. She told us that there was good news and bad news. The good news was that on Friday she had spoken to the Czech's solicitor, and he had agreed together with the Czech that tomorrow would be fine to complete. The Czech hadn't flown over after all, and was awaiting word from his solicitor as to the best time for him to come over. A bluff, huh we knew it!!! He planned to coincide his business here, together with the signing of any contracts. Hence, Martina hadn't completed the contracts yet. So much for his deadline! It was great news for us though. It bought us the extra time we so desperately needed- though it would have been nice if someone had told us of this change of plans, then perhaps we wouldn't have been so worried, and might not have had to carry these bags under our eyes all morning. It was good news nevertheless. The bad news was that there had still been no news from the Arab's solicitor regarding coming to the Land Registry with us, and getting the title deeds transferred into our names. Shit! Martina was going to chase her some more, so once again it was out of our hands. We'd just have to wait!!!

The next to call was Alexia. As per usual, wanting to interrogate us as to what was happening, as if we knew! It was needless to say a very awkward conversation on our part, knowing that we might actually be pulling out of her deal in favour of another. But that's the risk she took for not getting a reservation deposit! At two o'clock we finally received a call from our very own phantom, Anthony! He explained how he had been over the North gambling which is why he had not received our calls. Oh cheers very much we thought. Thanks for letting us wait all day yesterday! We informed him once again of our situation, that the contracts were being drawn up with the Czech as we speak, and that we would be signing them tomorrow. We urged him that we needed confirmation and a reservation fee from his client A.S.A.P. "No problem," he replied confidently as only accomplished Estate Agents can. He said the deal was definitely still on. His client would be over in the next couple of hours to sort it all out. Once again our hopes were raised. It appeared as if we had been granted a last minute reprieve.

Without delay, we rushed once more back to Titanic and tidied up, yet again, in preparation for his client and our new buyer to come. Our hopes began to waver slightly once two hours had come and gone. However, still, we kept the faith like two blind believers. Then three hours passed then four. Before we knew it the whole day had been stolen away from us and night time had once more crept up. No sign or word from anyone! No calls of apology or explanation. Nothing, a big fat zero! Yet again! It seemed that as mysteriously as he had appeared, he had vanished. Like a thief in the night, stealing peoples time and patience. Sprinkling yet more complication and confusion into an already complicated and confused situation. Truly a Phantom! Maybe even the very same Phantom that all of the rumours are forged from. I know that none of the above can possibly make any sense to you, the reader. After all, as Dr Spock would say "there's no logic to it!" All I can say in our defence, is that we have not made these events up. It all happened just as I have written it!

On hindsight after giving this whole episode much thought, we have come to the following conclusion. We now believe that our Phantom was actually induced by ourselves. That, in fact, we were having a joint hallucination brought about by all the mental stresses and strains that we were under at the time. You see just before the phantom appeared we desperately needed a boost, a quick fix to pick us up and a boost was exactly what our phantom gave us, brief as it was. However, if our Phantom was not an hallucination and was truly for real, then I can honestly say that he is absolutely without doubt one of the strangest Estate Agents we have ever met, and my advice to you is watch out for him!!! If he ever appears at your door DO NOT let him in whatever you do, no matter what smooth words he weaves at you, because if you do, he'll mess with your mind so badly that by the time he's finished. you'll not know your left from your right, your up from your down. Heed our story and beware of him. The one they call…"THE PHANTOM!!!"

CHAPTER 19

Chaos Central

On Tuesday, there had still been no communication with the Arab's solicitor. Still no time had been set for us to get the title deeds transferred. Not good news to speak of at all! Despite this, Martina was continuing with the contracts. They had now prepared both contracts, the immovable contract, which just to remind you is the Contract of Sale for the actual apartment itself, and the movable Contract of Sale, which is for the furnishings etc. As we said before, the movable items are not subject to tax. For this reason it is better for the vendor if this one is substantial. In our case, it was for thirty thousand pounds. If you take into consideration the twenty percent capital gains tax that would be incurred on this amount if it were included as part of the immovable sale price, then in real terms separating it equated to a saving of six thousand pounds, although having said that, we had spent a lot furnishing the property so this would come out of our profit here. From the buyer's point of view, a lower sale price for the immovable property equated to a lower transfer fee for them when they come to transferring the title deeds into their names.

It is however, a disadvantage if they ever decide to sell, as they will, on paper appear to have bought the property for just the immovable contract price. It is worse if you are unlucky enough to have purchased the property with a split contract, and then when it comes to selling your buyer refuses to sign one with you. You would then ultimately incur more on the books profit, and thus be liable to more capital gains tax. Something to beware of! However, it really is standard practice in Cyprus to do split contracts, so this situation is not one that should occur very often unless you're unlucky.

With all the uncertainty of our sale still hovering over our heads like a rain cloud about to fall, we decided to go out and spend some of the money that we didn't have on a fish mezze down by the sea. A good meal always cheers us up so it seemed like a good idea at the time. The sun was out, as usual ☺ and the view was fantastic. For a while we had forgotten all about the whole sorry affair, and were both enjoying our selection of fine fish that was being endlessly served up to us. That is until the mobile phone interrupted our moment of peace. It was a call from Martina. Yet another problem had raised it's ugly head! She had drafted up the contracts and Andonas, the Czech's solicitor, had finally read through them. The problem was that he wasn't happy about the split contract. He said that due to the fact that we would save six thousand pounds if his client signed the split contract, it was only fair that we split the saving with them. In short he wanted us to give them three thousand pounds off the sale price, otherwise he would recommend his client not to sign the split contract. Suddenly our meal tasted off! We were furious, and both adamant, that we would not sell our property for a penny less. After all the running around we had done to push this deal through, even without a deposit of any kind. As far as we were concerned, it was a damned cheek.

We decide to tell Martina about our other offer. We told her to tell him that at this stage, with another offer on the table, it was take it or leave it time. Finally, we had got tough. Of course we didn't tell Martina that our other offer had gone A.W.O.L, or about our Phantom. We were of course bluffing, but were so pissed off with the Czech's threats that we didn't really care if the whole deal did fall through.

Ten minutes later Martina called back and told us that in the light of the other offer Andonas had rethought his position, and had agreed to sign the split contract as it was. He also hadn't actually read the list of furniture we provided with the contract and though it was all pure profit – not that that's any of his business! A wave of relief swept over us as all out nuclear war had been successfully avoided. If nothing else we must thank our Phantom for giving us the leverage we needed to deal with the likes of Andonas, even if it was all a bluff ☺.

After this latest example of trying to take advantage of the situation, we were growing to dislike the Czech, and more precisely his solicitor Andonas, more and more and would have loved nothing more than for our Phantom to come through for us with his new buyer. But this is the real world that we live in, and at this stage our Czech was all we had!

It wasn't until the next day that Martina finally got a date off the Arab's solicitor to transfer the title deeds into our names. We had an appointment set at the Land registry office for Friday morning at eight thirty a.m. If our Czech was still with us by then we could finally get on and conclude the deal. We would just have to cross our fingers and hope for Friday to come quickly.

Like true Brits we arrived at the Land Registry Office spot on eight thirty, as arranged. Needless to say, this was an important "appointment" for us and we didn't want to miss it. Not after the time and effort it had taken us to get to this stage. One small piece of advice, in Cyprus the word "appointment" doesn't have the same meaning as it does in the U.K. In Cyprus, it merely means be somewhere at around about a certain time, but does not actually mean that you have an arrangement to meet anyone at that certain time, as we soon found out! With our pockets stashed with cash, we turned up outside the doors of the land registry. Another word of advice for any would be bank robbers out there who happen to be reading this book! Forget banks! If you really want to make some serious cash, you'd be far better off turning over the Cyprus Land Registry Offices. I reckon there's more completely untraceable used notes flying around there than in any bank! You see, the land registry does not except cheques. Of course it does except Czechs just not cheques. Crazy but true! Everybody's wondering around warily with wads of cash ready to pay off their relevant taxes and fees. One more word of advice for you, if you see some free seats, grab them. Trust me you'll need them. I think it's a running joke that the staff at the land registry offices have. They only provide enough seats for approximately half the amount of people there are likely to be. We were the lucky ones and managed to get a couple of seats, but what must have been no more than five minutes after we had arrived, there were no more seats to be had not for love nor money. Twenty minutes later, the entire room was as packed as rush hour on the Northern Line. Land Registry Office, Huh! We were in the heart of Chaos Central!

Our contact was a woman called Mariana. She had P.O.A to deal with this matter on behalf of the Arab's solicitor. It is what these people do. They act on behalf of various law firms down at the land registry office. Basically the law firms pay them to deal with their cases down at the land registry office, thus saving them the time it takes to get things done down there, and believe you me it takes a long, long time!!! We know this now but at the time we didn't really understand the ins and outs of her service. When we finally met her about an hour later, she was stacked up with at least ten other people's paperwork as well as ours. Surrounded by other applicants she acknowledged our presence with a nod, and told us to wait for her call. So wait we did. After all waiting was something we were becoming experts at! One last piece of advice for you, if you happen ever to have to go to the land registry office yourselves, pack a lunch and some drinks because you could be in for a long wait!

At eleven o'clock Mariana called us up. Our time had come. All our waiting was finally over. We hacked a route over to her through the crowd, where she had us sign a couple of documents, then to our shock she told us to sit back down and wait. We tried to ask her what was going on, or if she had any idea of how much longer we could expect to wait. At least if she told us that we could have got a drink or something instead of being chained to our seats fearful of missing our call. Because trust me they do not call twice! But she said nothing, just gestured us to go away and stop bothering her! So not wishing to upset her, we obeyed and went back to our waiting. Not to our chairs, since by now they had both been snapped up by other fellow waiters whose chair train had just arrived.

We sat and watched like two huge yellow lemons as the room slowly emptied. As the sun moved from one side to the other. However, when finally we were summoned it appeared that our luck was in. We weren't the last to get seen, we were the second to last! I can remember watching the last remaining couples' envious eyes tracking us as we followed Mariana like two little puppy dogs following their mum. It was now three o'clock in the afternoon, and Mariana led us out of the waiting area and up to the main offices on the first floor. It was in this section of Chaos Central where we were to meet the judicators in this lottery or "Super Bingo" as they have in Cyprus, that they call transfer fees. Unbeknown to us it was here that we would have to present our case to them and pray for leniency as they determine in their infinite wisdom the worth of our property. Forget the actual price that we paid for the property. The actual price stated on our contract of sale. All that "actual" stuff means absolutely nothing at Chaos Central! No, it's all down to the judicator's verdict as to how much money they decide you're property is worth so you'd better take some extra cash with you just to be safe. Something unfortunately we didn't do. We had brought the exact amount to cover the transfer fee which we had calculated from our exact purchase price stated on our contract of sale. We were told that most of the time they calculate it on a lower purchase price so if we were lucky we might have to pay less but no one told us that we might have to pay more! I know what you're thinking. Why not simply calculate the amount of transfer fee you have to pay on the exact price stated on your contract of sale? A crazy, radical idea, that just might work. An idea, that would mean there would be no need for judicators or judges. Well we had the same idea. The only answer I've got in response to that idea is, don't be so bloody stupid! I mean this is Cyprus after all ☺.

Outside the judicator's room were yet more people. People we recognised from the waiting room downstairs, now waiting here instead of there, just as we were going to have to. Mariana pointed to the chairs and signalled us to wait once more. As we sat the yells and screams from inside the judicator's office echoed down the hallway ominously. We couldn't understand the Greek words that were being yelled but you didn't have to be fluent in Greek to understand their meaning. These people inside were clearly unhappy with whatever amount they were being asked to pay. Not a good sign for us, we thought!

Finally, one hour later we were summoned, by the judicator himself, into his office. He was a short, stocky little man and his office was as most government offices are, grim! No state of the art flat screen monitors here, or fresh coats of white paint. Judging by the faded paint that had been tarnished from the years of direct sunlight and smoker's smoke, this office was well used and under funded. Ironical, since this office probably earned the government a fortune. Anyway, he sat us down on the other side of his small desk and Mariana, who had followed us inside presented him with our documents. As she placed them on his desk he let out a tired sigh. This man was clearly not in the best of moods after his shouting match with the people before us.

"You have your Contract of Sale?" he muttered, as he scanned the documents that Mariana had just given him. It almost appeared an effort for him to speak. Lara pulled it out from our rucksack and presented it to him. Once again he let out another sigh, this time louder and longer than the last, as he took the Contract of Sale from Lara. He browsed over it and rubbed his chin. Then he looked up to us and said, "So it's a sea front apartment? Hmm!" He reached back to a large filing cabinet behind him, and rummaged through it. A red book came out of one of the files and he flicked through the pages. Then he peered up at us once more, "Looking at these past sales in your block I would value your apartment at sixty-five thousand pounds." This was of course a complete shock for us both and not good news.

"But as you can see we only paid fifty-five thousand pounds," we replied.

"I'm sorry but as I just said, judging from previous sales in your block, it is worth sixty five thousand pounds and therefore I must tax you on that amount!"

Suddenly, it was all too clear what was happening here. He was as he kept saying, judging our apartment by others in the same block. What he wasn't taking into consideration was that ours was in a far worse state of neglect than any of the other apartments that he was comparing ours too and therefore, could not possibly be worth as much. It was right in the midst of all of this when Mariana threw into the mix yet more confusion. We thought that she was about to say something helpful, boy were we wrong!

"Oh yes," she said to us from the corner of the room where

she was lurking like a bad smell, "there's also the small matter of the unpaid bills for the apartment."

This was news to us. "What unpaid bills?" we enquired curiously.

"Don't worry we've already paid them on your behalf but we've been instructed that we must get the money back from you."

We really didn't have a clue what she was talking about, and quite honestly with us being right in the middle of dealing with the tax man, this was really not the time for her to be bringing whatever this was up! But bring it up she had, so the question had to be asked.

"There were outstanding bills to the amount of five hundred and ninety six pounds. They are for the sewage and general municipality bills."

"What bills? We've been paying all of our bills!" needless to say our stress levels were beginning to rise. "What dates are these bills for?"

"These bills are going back to 1994."

"You've got to be joking!" we both exclaimed, "We've only bought the apartment in March 2005!"

"I'm sorry but I have my instructions that I must get the money from you!"

She was a heartless cow who was clearly taking advantage of the fact that we were right in the thick of things, and were probably less likely to be thinking straight. If ever a similar thing happens to you, do not pay it. It will be stipulated in your Contract of Sale that any outstanding bills, up to the date of the sale must be paid by the previous owner, not by you. As we had only owned it since March, and these bills were stretching back to '94, Mariana was obviously trying to take advantage of the situation. There was no excuse for her since she knew the law better than anyone else. It was part of their job, after all.

Of course at this moment in time we were under stress and very confused, so although we knew that we should not pay all of these bills, we were not sure if we should pay some of it. We waved her back and continued with the matter at hand with the tax man. Fortunately for us, Lara had the foresight to have printed up some before pictures that clearly showed the original state of the apartment. You know what they say, pictures can say more than a thousand words and with them you can be sure that nothing gets lost in translation. So we explained to him that our purchase price was lower because of the terrible condition that the apartment was in, after years of neglect. Lara pulled out the pictures to show him. If he was unsure before as soon as he saw the pictures he'd be sure to see our point.

"Daxi!" he muttered as he curiously examined the pictures, "and you still brought this apartment?" he said with a slight smile. A tax man with a sense of humour, a rare sight indeed! "Look the best I can do is sixty thousand pounds."

It was five thousand better, but still more than we had actually paid. Who would have thought that we'd be haggling in a tax office over the price? Certainly not something that would ever happen in England ☺.

Lara began to plea some more with him, as it was clear he was softening up a little. Maybe he had been weakened by the previous screamers, who knows? "But we've had to spend so much on it to fix it," Lara said, "Look we've done the roof, completely re-plumbed it, new water tanks, new kitchen, new everything!"

"Look I tell you what I can do. If you can show me all your receipts I'll let it go for the fifty five thousand."

"That's great. We've got all the receipts so there's no problem there," Lara answered excitedly. It seemed at long last we were getting somewhere.

"Can I see them?" he asked.

His words stumped us. Although we did have all the receipts we hadn't brought them with us. We didn't realise that we might need them. "We haven't got them with us," Lara replied.

"O.K. Come back next week with your receipts and we can settle it then." This was even worst news for us. We had to settle it today. Next week was going to be too late. If we didn't get this permission today we could kiss goodbye to our sale. "Please! Look we have to conclude this today," I pleaded desperately hoping he would be lenient.

"I'm sorry but without those receipts the best I can do is sixty thousand pounds."

"How about fifty seven thousand, because we only have enough money on us to cover the tax on that amount?" As I mentioned we had brought the exact amount we calculated on the value being fifty-five thousand pounds, but for some reason, lucky to us, his calculations seem to bring the tax due slightly lower, so this still came under our budget.

"What you didn't bring anymore?"

"We only thought that we would have to pay fees on the contract of sale price." With that comment he just gave out a huge almighty laugh that said, "You two really are naive aren't you?" He then thought for a few seconds rubbing his chin some more and scanned over the pictures again. Then he looked up at us.

"O.K. Fifty-seven thousand pounds but you must bring those receipts into me next week." And so the deal was done. We were relatively happy and he signed off the rest of the documents, and worked out the transfer fees that we had to pay. We swiftly shook hands and vacated the office before he had time to change his mind. Now all that was left to do was pay the fees and get our receipt. There was still the issue of these bills that needed to be sorted, as Mariana was eager to remind us when we were paying our fees downstairs. We told her that there was no way we were going to pay all of it, since we had only owned it since March. We told her we'd pay our share of this year's bill only, which they worked out to be one hundred pounds. In hind sight our share of one year's sewage bill was less than that but to keep the peace we paid it anyway. Then, just as we were in the middle of counting through the money that we were giving to the cashier, she slapped us with a final insult.

"Oh yes," she croaked. "There's also the matter of my fees." This was yet again news to us. Up until now we had thought that she was part of the government department, assigned to help us in these issues. We had no idea that we had employed her services. "My fees are thirty pounds." Her words were timed to perfection, just as we had a huge wadge of notes fanned out in our hands. Like a true couple of mugs, we paid her not wishing to upset anyone or sound stupid, after all it had been a long day. I did ask her for a receipt however. She said she didn't have one on her. Surprising really, since she was clearly thoughtful of her fees. The best she would do was to scribble down the amount she had received on a scrap piece of paper. Hardly worth the paper it was written on. Anyway, after a whole day and a heap of stress leading up to it, we were finally handed our all important receipt- the yellow receipt that proved our names were going to be on the title deeds. Receiving the actual title deeds was now just a formality that would take about a month.

Walking out of the land registry, receipt firmly in hand, we couldn't help but ponder over the day. Specifically Marianas roll in it! It just didn't seem correct us having to pay her thirty pounds, and the more we thought about her demands for us to pay the previous bills the more it began to grit in our teeth. Later, when we had a bit more time to work it out and our heads were a bit clearer, we worked out that our share of this years bills should not have come up to the one hundred pounds and sure enough, after speaking to Martina, she confirmed Mariana should not have charged us thirty pounds. She was actually representing the Arab's solicitor at the Land registry, and not us. Which, when we thought about it, made complete sense. After all, if she had been representing us, then we would not have had to be there ourselves in the first place. We wouldn't have had to waste our entire day waiting. Since she was representing the Arab's solicitor, it should have been her who should have been picking up the bill and not us. Something, we're quite sure Mariana knew perfectly well.

We have since found out that this is a little scam that Mariana has had going for quite a few years. The probability is that our Mariana is playing both sides. Getting employed and paid by one side, then taking extra cash where she can off the unsuspecting mugs like us on the other side, who don't know any better. This leads us to the question of, how many other people is she regularly doing this to? I'm sure as hell we weren't the only ones and won't be the last. There were at least four other English people there whose cases she was handling. Not to mention the ten or more other cases that she had under her arm. Most of them I'm sure, if asked, would just pay the money not thinking anything of it, fly back to the U.K. or wherever else they've come from, completely oblivious to the fact that they've just been tangoed by our very own Mariana. How much extra cash was this little scam pulling in for her every year? I guess we'll never know, but one thing's for sure. As far as I'm concerned it was thirty pounds well spent, although I confess we weren't thinking that at the time. I mean education doesn't come cheap, not at the University of Life! At least now thanks to our mentor Mariana, we'll never fall for that one again, and now hopefully, neither will you.

As I said, at the time we were understandably furious and wanted to head back to confront Mariana to get our money back. Fortunately, Martina talked us out of it. She explained how it probably wasn't such a good idea, since the likes of Mariana have their mitts into everything. Contacts everywhere, in all the government departments. She told us how someone like Mariana could make life very difficult for us, and that it was best to drop it and put it down to experience. Of course she was right. However, she didn't tell me not to put it in this book. Probably because she didn't know I was writing it. So my advice to you is this, if ever anyone asks you for money that you weren't aware you were ever meant to pay, don't! If you're not sure about it then delay them. Find out more and pay them later, only if of course you're satisfied that they should be paid. Even better if you have a good solicitor ring them first and ask them what they think you should do. I'm sure if we had taken our own advice Mariana would not have got a penny out of us and we could have gone out and had a nice three course meal with the money we had saved. Oh well! ☹

Anyway, we dropped the receipt off with Martina who with it could now proceed with the final contracts and then headed back to Titanic and crashed. We were glad to finally have everything in place that we needed to complete. If nothing else, our day at Chaos Central made us vow that in future, we would employ the services ourselves of someone like Mariana, and let them spend the day waiting at the land registry office while we do something more productive with our time like, playing tennis ☺.

CHAPTER 20

The Exchange

As you would expect the next day we had mail from Martina. Apparently there was a problem. Not another one we thought. The Czech's solicitor, Andonas, now wasn't happy with the receipt we had obtained. The news came as follows:

From: Martina
Sent: 12 December 2005 16:16
To: Pete & Lara
Subject: Contract

Dear Pete & Lara,

I had a call from Andonas and he told me the following: on Friday he had the same situation in the Land Registry Office: the transfer has been just executed and a title yet to be issued and the application for the deposit of the Sale contract has been rejected by the Land Registry. I haven't ever heard of such kind of procedure. But, anyway these restrictions may exist?

In this respect his position is:
1. To sign the contracts on Monday in any case
2. To pay approximately CYP 10.000 and obtain the possession

of the flat and the rest of the amount to pay upon the issuance of the title (**Not on your Nelly mate!!!**) OR

3. To pay a deposit of CYP 1.000 only and the rest of the amount upon the issuance of the title deed. In this case you will not delivery the possession of the flat till full settlement of the purchase price.

In any case the funds will be transferred to Andonas's account and kept there till the title is issued.

Actually, this will be discussed tomorrow between the Andonas and his client.

I do not know what option is preferable for you. But, this will depend as well on the meeting between Andonas and his Client. *(Needless to say option one is preferable to us at this stage thank you ☺)*

On Monday I have a meeting with Andonas at 11.30. And after this takes place I will give you a call to arrange the time for signing.

Sincerely yours,

Martina
Advocate

Quite frankly, in our opinion, Andonas was being a complete arsehole. He knew that we were getting the receipt and had up to now been quite happy with it. Obviously, the actual title deeds would not come through for at least a month. That being the case there were two issues that I could see: Firstly, I don't think our nerves had a month left in them and secondly, would the Czech be prepared to wait for yet another month? This seemed to us at this stage highly debatable. However, this time there was really nothing else we could do other than to once again wait!!!

Our much anticipated call from Martina came through on the Monday at about twelve thirty. She had just finished her meeting with the infamous Andonas. This time she brought good news. The deal was on ☺ Hallelujah!!! Praise the lord. Finally sense had prevailed. The Czech had decided that he was quite prepared to except our receipt as proof of ownership and proceed with the signing of contracts. I think we had finally worn him down. Martina had arranged a signing time of four o'clock, as long as it was O.K with us. A stupid question really, as we would have been willing to sign these contracts at any time of day or night. Andonas had insisted that the signing take place in his office and not Martina's. There was a bit of male ego lawyer stuff going on but again this was completely agreeable to us. Anywhere would do, even Timbuktu just as long as we finally got these damned contracts signed, sealed and delivered. And as the Americans put it "get closure" on this whole sordid affair! So the place and time had been set now, all we had to do was turn up with our pens. This was the moment that we had been dreaming of. The moment that up till now we were starting to believe would never happen.

Martina, Lara and I waltzed into the offices of Andonas four o'clock sharp. Anna had in her possession all of the contracts to be signed, which she had painstakingly prepared personally. I think at this stage she herself was looking forward to finally getting some closure on this case too. Andonas's office was a world apart from Martina's. No Ally McBeal type woman power here. No feminine niceties like fresh flowers or bright modern colour coordination. Here it was strictly a male affair. Typical old school Cypriot. Here the women were nothing more than receptionists there to look pretty, take calls and offer refreshments when needed. The reception walls were filled with law books stacked from top to bottom. Books of many different shapes, sizes and colours and I can only presume that since they were behind the receptionist's desk, were never used and clearly for show. Maybe their real use was to inform us, the uneducated peasants, of just how knowledgeable these people really were. So that we would be in awe of them right from the off set, who knows? From an interior designer's point of view the only thing they said to us was clutter!

We were ushered into the meeting room by the receptionist who surprise, surprise offered us all refreshments. The Czech was already in there sitting by himself on one side of the huge oak meeting table that filled the room, but no Andonas. Lara pulled up a seat at one end of the table, and Martina and I sat opposite the Czech leaving the seat at the head of the table for Andonas. We were just guests after all! To a fly on the wall, it must have appeared as if this was some sort of multinational million pound business takeover that was about to take place in such lavish surroundings, not a mere one hundred and eighteen thousand pound apartment sale.

The receptionist came in with our drinks just in the nick of time, as the conversation began to dry up between us and the Czech. After all there's really only so much you can say to a man you have grown to despise! A few sips latter and finally we were graced with the man himself. The one, the only, Andonas!!!

Andonas was your typical alpha male Cypriot lawyer. Completely suited and booted from head to toe with the finest cloth. He could have been an Estate Agent ☺. He was tall, dark and loathsome and strutted in as if he were on the set of Night Fever, overflowing with testosterone.

"Hello everyone. Sorry I'm late." he said unconvincingly as he sat down at the head of the table. He reached over and firmly shook my hand introducing himself to me but barely acknowledged Lara or Martina. Then he proceeded with business swiftly handing out to everyone copies of the contracts that Martina had created.

"O.K. everyone here are the contracts I've prepared," he said. All three of us looked at each other in disbelief, as he blatantly took credit for Martina's hard work. Of course the Czech thought he was amazing, clearly impressed with Andonas's apparent efficiently. Martina sat silently with complete professionalism, bit her lip and said nothing. However, her eyes said it all. The meeting continued. On reading through the contract that had been presented to us, sure enough it was the exact same one we had already seen. All seemed to be in order on that front. It had been agreed before hand, something Andonas had insisted on, that three thousand pounds would be held back until a tax clearance certificate had been received.

The tax clearance certificate is issued when all the outstanding taxes i.e. capital gains tax, council tax etc. have been paid. Until these taxes are paid the next owners can not get the title deeds transferred into their names. Apparently, it was a simple case (if there is ever such a thing in Cyprus!) of going down to the tax offices with our contracts of sale, both our original purchase one to show the price we brought the property for, and this new one to show the price we had sold it for. Also we would have to take all of our receipts etc. and then as with the land registry present our case. As with the land registry it seemed that the amount of tax we'd have to pay would be dependant on what mood the tax officer was in! In theory, with the amount we had spent on the property, combined with the fact that there is a one off exemption from capital gains tax on the first ten thousand pounds for each person currently granted, we had worked out that we would not have to pay any tax this time around. However, after our land registry experience, this time we were keeping more of an open mind.

Anyway we were fine with this point, but then Andonas threw into the mix one more demand which we had not been informed of. He wanted us to sign P.O.A over to him to give him the right to act on our behalf when it came to the final transfer of the title deeds. Usually, after all the taxes have been cleared and everyone was ready to get the title deeds transferred, both the purchaser and previous owner, have to go down together to the land registry office. There are additional forms that require our signatures at this stage. Andonas's reasoning for wanting P.O.A in this matter, was that we might not still be in the country and therefore could slow this procedure down when it came to this stage. He had prepared (although whether he himself had actually prepared it was for obvious reasons dubious!) a small one page P.O.A document for us to sign.

We really weren't very happy about having to give him P.O.A and told him so. Our reasoning was that there was no need for him to have it, since we were currently living in the country and could therefore come at any time when required to sign any forms that needed to be signed. However on this issue he was adamant. So we all read through his P.O.A, Martina included. Martina confirmed that it was entirely specific and only gave him P.O.A on this issue so reluctantly we signed. Andonas took the signed contracts back and casually told us that he'd get copies sent over to us in the morning.

At that remark, Martina responded, and quite rightly so, "No. We need copies now Andonas."

"You might as well wait 'till tomorrow when they'll all be stamped," he replied smugly; all official documents have to be stamped by a notary to validate them. "Then you'll just have to give us copies of these ones now and copies of the stamped ones later Andonas." Martina replied firmly.

It was completely crazy for him to even suggest us going away without copies of what we had just signed. There are two golden rules where contracts are concerned: 1) always read through them thoroughly- something so simple but alas, something that many people fail to do, and 2) always take away copies of any contracts that you have just signed. If you don't have copies then anything could be altered inside them without your knowledge! Andonas was clearly vexed at Martina's response. It eroded away at his male ego. He regained his composure and laughed the matter off, desperately trying to regain face by telling us that Martina was just protecting our interests. Deerrrr!!! We both thought. Of course she is, after all, she is our lawyer.

He called his receptionist in and instructed her to make copies. After all, copying files would have been completely beneath such a man as Andonas! With our copies in hand, the meeting was finally concluded and our sale was complete. It was agreed that the money, all one hundred and fifteen thousand, would be transferred into our account in the morning, after which we would gladly hand over the keys to the Czech.

As we left, Andonas once again shook my hand as if we were best friends, but merely nodded to Lara and Martina in vague acknowledgment. What a creep! I couldn't help but feel for Martina. How hard it must be for a woman like her in such a male dominated country. Martina, an intelligent woman, who can speak Russian, Greek & English all fluently. Passing with honours law degrees, not only in her native Russian language, but then again in Greek but always having to humour idiots such as Andonas who still believe that a woman's place is in the home. Cyprus is certainly not an easy place for career woman, but hopefully it will slowly catch up with the rest of Europe! Miracles do happen!

The walk back to the car was blissful. It was as if we had just won a huge war. We dropped Martina off at her car outside her law firm. As we said our goodbyes we pulled out from the back of the pick-up, a huge hamper all wrapped up in ribbons and bows to give to her. We had purchased it before the meeting and were only too happy to give it to her, in appreciation for all of her hard work. Lara hugged Martina and broke into tears. All of her pent up emotions over this whole drawn out affair had finally been released. It was at last over, well bar the last three thousand. As of tomorrow we were going to be back in the money and as far as we were concerned, well rid of our first project. A project that despite all of its difficulties, we had miraculously managed to pull a good profit in on. It was ironical to think that at one point we would have been quite happy to have given it away.

That evening we cleared all of our things out from the apartment. We hoped to slip out of there like ninjas, without anyone ever knowing we had left. No farewells, and certainly no goodbyes, just good riddance! Of course, we did leave for the Czech the hose, the mop and dust pan, stacked neatly in one of the cupboards compliments of us. No instructions though, we figured the Czech would learn soon enough what they were for! It was amazing just how much stuff we had in there. All of which added to the existing clutter in our small two bed that we were going to have to move back into.

But believe you me, the cons outweighed the pros as far as we were concerned, and as we shut the door of Titanic behind us, there were no tears spilled and certainly no regrets, just pure joy!!! As we rode the crappy lift down and walked out of the foyer I felt like shouting out at the top of my voice, "Do what you will, you miserable f**ers. The elves have left the building!!!" No more worrying about their graffiti or their rubbish. No more worrying about the roof and the rain, or people not paying their maintenance. We were well out of it. I couldn't help but wonder how long it would be before the Czech realised that a great view ain't everything? Oh well, it was his problem now. Sure enough the money went into our account first thing the very next morning, and we handed him the keys that afternoon. He still seemed over the moon at his purchase and overwhelmed by the view. Who were we to shatter his dream?

Obtaining our tax clearance certificate proved to be not quite as simple as we were led to believe. We went into the tax office stacked up with all of our receipts, only to be informed that most of them we could not use. Their reason was as follows. Apparently, you can only deduct from your profit the cost of the value of any additions. Confused? Well so were we! I'll try to simplify it for you. If, for example, your house does not have any stairs and you put new stairs, in then the total cost of the stairs can be deducted. If you're property already has floor tiling worth £5, and you replace the existing tiling with new and more expensive floor tiling worth £10 then you can only claim back the difference of £5. Once again, this was a perfect example of crazy Cypriot logic and once again, it's down to the discretion of the particular tax officer you happen to come across. For obvious reasons, this is not so good if like us, you are renovating old run down properties as under this scheme you can not claim back all the works you would have done like replacing an old bathroom suite or kitchen.

Fortunately, if you are doing it through a business you can claim the additional receipts back through that. Besides all of the above, all the forms that we needed to fill out were of course in Greek. We were forced to retreat and come back with a representative acting on our behalf. He filled out all the forms for us and knew exactly how to play the system. He put Lara down as a house-wife and me down as a telephone engineer. He told us to say that we had brought the property as a holiday home and that our reason for selling was due to the fact that the building was terrible. That much was true. The aim was to make the tax officer feel sorry for us. It seemed to work as he allowed £20k

CYP of our receipts through, and sure enough together with our tax allowance we did not have to pay any capital gains tax, this time! Our tax clearance receipt was issued and our final £3k CYP was successfully received. The deal was done and truly dusted.

Looking back, I think the first project is always destined to be the most painful. After all on this one you're like little spotty apprentices fresh out of school. It's this first one where you do all of your learning, mostly the hard way! To make matters worse it's the one you have the least amount of money to spare and in our case, it was combined with the fact that we were in a new and foreign country, which in itself is difficult to put it mildly. However, we had proved something very important to ourselves, and to others and that was that we could do it and do it well. We had proved that renovations were certainly something that we could make a living out of. Of course next time we'd do a few things differently, but overall we had succeeded.

With this project under our belts, we were now surer than ever that rentals were definitely not for us. It was time to focus in on what was making us money and get rid of what clearly wasn't, and that was our rental apartments!!! Both the Agia Napa studios and the ever ominous Fuller Paphos off plans, which were creeping ever nearer to that dreaded 75% build stage, at which point we were going to be asked for the next 60% of the cash. If we weren't careful, it could be a case of "in one hand and out the other!" So our game plan was to get the two Agia Napa studios up for sale, and find out what was happening with the Fuller off plans, as up to now we had heard not so much as a whisper regarding them from Fuller ! It was time to shoot a mail off to them and find out exactly what was going on with them...

CHAPTER 21

Fuller Shite!!!

It was a couple of days before we had a response back from Fuller. The response we had was not good. They told us that our apartments were currently up for sale and worst of all, the next 60% would indeed be due by the end of January. There was no more information than that so needless to say it was time to hook up a meeting with them to find out exactly what was going on in more detail, and what our options were. I made the call and a meeting was arranged for the next day at the Limassol branch.

We entered into the Fuller office and were met by Dawn, the starry-eyed Northern rep. It seemed as if the glory days of the Jed era that we had remembered had alas long since passed. The office was completely deserted. No hustle and bustle of agents busy selling their shite. It was a case of, "and then there was one!" She welcomed us in as all good agents do, as if we were her bosom buddies.

"Hi ya," she said as she pulled up a couple of chairs for us both in front of her desk. We couldn't help but wonder, as we looked at her from across her desk, whether these agents were actually manufactured in some sort of agent factory. I mean, they all seemed to look the same. They were all about mid forties with northern accents. Makeup was always a meter thick, possibly designed for them to hide behind when the going gets tough- who knows? I had images of the Omen film in my head. I imagined that if I held her head down on the desk, and Lara moved aside her hair instead of 666 marked on her scalp, we'd probably find "Made in Taiwan." Judging by the look on her face I reckon she was having the exact same thought about us. The only difference being that when she moved our hair aside she would find the word "MUGS" written on our scalps. I guess we'll never know. Anyway, once we were all seated she continued with her trivial crap, possibly trying to sweeten us up before we raised our real questions, the ones that were clearly on our minds like ten ton bricks threatening to fall.

"So how are you both?" she continued, "You must be so happy after selling Titanic? You did a great job of it, we all thought so in the office."

I think she was quite content talking to herself. I had to interject and guide her back on course. "Look Dawn. As our email stated, we need to know what's happening with our Fuller off-plans?" She was suddenly silenced and her caked face briefly dropped, as if she had just been struck by a killing question. She quickly remembered her agent training, and raised her smile back up to its original fakeness. But the telltale signs of stress were clearly there, as a droplet of sweat broke through her foundation and dribbled down the side of her face.

"Oh yes your Fuller projects. That's right they're coming up to the 75% build stage, and the next 60% is going to be due this month," she tapped on her keyboard and viewed her screen, "yes I can see that they are currently listed for £40,500."

"That's right," I answered as she peered at me vaguely, "Our questions to you are as follows:

1: How come no one told us that these projects were coming up to 75% build stage? We were only up there in August and the site was still nothing but dirt!

2: We saw for ourselves that they are up for sale on the Fuller website but who told you to list them because we certainly didn't?

3: It just so happens that we do wish to sell these two studios, but we did not give you the price we wanted to sell them at so how did you get the figures that they are currently up for? It seems a vastly overpriced figure for two 30m^2 studios, especially since you can get the equivalent studios in Agia Napa for only £28000 CYP.

4: Most importantly, how long have they been listed for sale?

5: How many in our project have currently been resold? After all, the projects were specifically sold to us on the assumption that Fuller would sell them on before we had to pay the next 60% instalment."

By the fifth question the dribble had turned into a torrent. Her stretched fake smile was in serious danger of snapping. "Right!" she muttered clearly completely bemused. "Did you buy these off Jed?" Her question hit a raw nerve with us both that she could clearly see.

"Yes!" we both hissed in unison, clearly unimpressed.

"Yes, you see Jed was dealing with all the Fuller Paphos projects before he left. I don't really know the ins and outs of them, but I can tell you that we had a similar project here in Limassol and we had a real problem reselling them."

Alarm bells started to ring.

"You see the market has really dropped out here over the last year."

What happened to that twenty percent rise in the market that our mate Jed had assured us was going to take place, we wondered?

"Look, I haven't got all the answers but I'll give the main

office in Paphos a call and see if we can find out some more for you both," she said, head leant to one side and fake smile back in full force. Stepford wives eat your hearts out!

She made the call to the Paphos branch and these were the answers that followed. They said that the letter informing us of the approaching next instalment was probably sent to our old U.K. address. No explanation as to why there had been no email or phone call to us. There was no explanation given as to why our apartments were listed without our permission. After all, just maybe we didn't want to sell them? Apparently, the price they were listed for was thirty percent above our original purchase price. This was standard practice she told us, and something that Jed should have told us about. Well that was news to us and made absolutely no sense to us either. Surely it is down to us, the owners, as to what price we wish to sell our properties for and not the Estate Agents?

Since our properties were clearly already listed by Fuller, this was the question I really wanted answered. How long had they been listed for? I mean, as I said the price they had them listed for seemed rather excessive. However, you would assume that they knew what they were doing. But you know what they say, assumption is the mother of all f**k-ups! We could not believe the answer to this one. They had been listed at this same price for four months. The answer to question five was the final nail in the coffin as far as we were concerned. Up to now approximately none had been sold. Now call me crazy if you will but I would have thought that after four months of zero sales it would have been clear to any half decent sales person that the price was probably too high. Naturally we were furious to discover this news. It threw up more questions than answers. Dawn told us that she had heard of others whose apartments weren't selling, and they were being asked for the next 60% but could not afford it. After all, they had been sold them never expecting to have to come up with the next 60%. They, like us, and hopefully not like you, were told how easily they would sell at this stage. This was proving not to be the case, as now I'm quite sure Fuller had known all along.

The options in our contracts were to either pay the next 60% or pay the interest at 8% per annum. I could see real problems arising. Consider the fact that there are endless numbers of these new developments popping up all over the island like a bad case of measles- which there are! Clearly it seems that the market is saturated, so reselling is going to become more and more difficult to say the least. Now these investors, unable to sell at the 75% build stage, unable to pay the next 60% instalment because most of the suckers like us never banked on having to, and unable to even get a mortgage for the next instalment on these properties because they are not completed projects and as a result have no title deeds, or forced to pay more to the developers for a guarantee for the title deeds, will be forced to pay the 8% interest instead.

I, therefore, could also imagine that due to the fact that most of these investors are foreigners, a large proportion of them will say "screw you" and not pay the 8% interest, with the mind-set of "let the f***ers chase me for it and see how far they get!" This in turn will lead to a severe financial short fall and in turn would mean that the developers will not have the money to finish their projects. I could therefore, in the future, well imagine loads of unfinished developments scattered around the Cyprus landscape like scars. Just a thought!

Now our next issue was, considering that they had apparently been up for sale for the past four months, why on earth had the price not been lowered? Had no one thought of doing this? You could only think of two reasons why they would not have. Either they really had no real commitment to resell them, or they were completely stupid? Either way, obviously we wanted to reduce the price of ours straight away in order to stand more chance of selling. If anyone had bothered to inform us of the situation after a couple of months of them being listed, we would have had the price reduced a long time ago and would have maybe have sold them before now.

We could think of so many other things we would rather have our £40k CYP tied up in, and certainly didn't relish the thought of paying the 8% interest which was going to amount to approximately £3200 CYP per year. Not nice!!! So much for the, I quote *"Unique investment opportunity for the serious investor that can give potential returns on investment of more than 50% within a time frame of 12-18 months."* What a crock of old crap! We needed to sell them and fast. The joke was that in order to reduce the asking price, they insisted that we had to put it in writing. Well I'm sorry, but I don't remember them ever getting anything in writing off us to put the apartments up for sale at the price they were at in the first place. Perhaps it slipped our minds?

The other question we asked, was how are Fuller marketing our apartments? The answer was as we had suspected, not very well. We were told that they were of course up on their web site. Yeah, along with the other 200 pages of unsold Fuller apartments and developments. And let's be honest now, the chances of anyone even finding their site was 100 to one since it wasn't listed on any of the major search engines. None of these minor points seemed to deter our Dawn though, who was still on an up note as she told us how they are also with an English agent called George.

You couldn't imagine how relieved we were to hear that George from good old Blighty was on the case. All was not lost. If anyone could sell our apartments George could. Yeah right!!! Dawn also told us how we should get them listed with as many Estate Agents as possible over in Paphos. This seemed to be the first piece of good advice she gave us, not that we hadn't thought of it already! It was definitely time to get our apartments listed with everyone. We'd have to take a trip over to Paphos and get them listed with all the agents we possibly could over there if we were going to stand any chance of shifting them. At our new price the best we were hoping to do was to break even but at this stage, breaking even seemed like a good result.

Dawn sent our new asking price, in writing, off to head office and we were to await confirmation off them the next day. The next day confirmation came in the form of emails.

∽

From: Jane
Sent: 10 January 2006 17:41
To: Lara
Cc: Dawn
Subject: RE: Apts. 24 & 25 Fuller - Re-sale price reduction

Dear Lara & Pete,

I was concerned that the price you were proposing to re-sell at meant that you would suffer a loss. To show you the kind of deductions to expect, if you were to re-sell Apt. 24 @ CY £34,500 the calculations would be;

Apt. 24 — Proposed re-sale price:	34,500.00
5% sales commission to Fuller:	1,725.00-
1% legal fees:	345.00-
Cancellation of contract fee:	500.00-
	————————
Net price after deductions:'	CY £31,930.00
	————————

N.B. Based on the above formula, if you were to re-sell Apt. 25 for CY £33,500.00 the net figure after deductions would be CY £30,900.00

The above figures are based on your lawyer charging 1% for his services, which is I understand the standard legal fee for both selling and buying property in Cyprus. I am also assuming that neither of you will be liable to pay Capital Gains tax.
(***You must be taking the George F***ing Michael out of us. Capital gains tax? Huh. There's definitely not going to be any profit here!***)
Again this is something that you will need to check with your lawyer and if necessary increase the re-sale price accordingly to cover any such charges. *(***I think you've completely missed the point!!! The whole point is that they are clearly not selling and are clearly over priced.***)*

I await your confirmation that you wish us to advertise *(***that's a joke! ***)* your apartments for re-sale at the latest prices you have suggested in your email below. *(***Yes of course we do. It's the reason you insisted on it in writing!***)*

Best regards,

Jane

∽

From: Lara
Sent: 10 January 2006 16:58
To: Jane
Cc: Dawn
Subject: Apts. 24 & 25 Fuller - Re-sale price reduction

Hi Jane,

Thanks for your mail.

To be honest we are more interested in selling rather than waiting for a profit, so to confirm:

24 @ CY £34,500.00
25 @ CY £33,500.00

Hopefully this will still seem a good bargain to someone!!!

Look forward to hearing any responses!

thanks
Lara + Pete.

∽

At least now we had reduced our prices with them, for what good that would do! All that was left for us to do now was get over to Paphos and get them listed with the other agents. It seemed as if we were going to have to take a small loss on the Agia Napa studios too, if we were going to be able to sell them. They hadn't gone down in value but had not risen either. So taking into consideration all the inevitable fees etc. that would have to come off any sale, another loss was inevitable. Not much choice for us though. We either took a loss now or a long drawn out loss on the rentals, which weren't having the great returns that had been predicted by Jed. So definitely time to get them listed. And of course, lest we forget we still had our two bed apartment with all of its faults to get sorted. Another great Jed bargain.

There seemed to be one common factor (apart from us!) that linked together all of our crap buys, and that was Jed! God help anyone else who comes across him. Despite our victory on the Titanic front, we clearly still had a heck of a lot of Jed shite to clear up before we could truly relax out here. Not what we originally had in mind when we came out, but those were the cards that Jed had dealt us, and unfortunately the cards that we had taken!!! We figured it was time to use good old Jed for us, rather than against us. If anyone could sell all of this crap that we had he could. After all, he sold it to us! As I've said before, unfortunately Estate Agents are a necessary evil and we needed to get with as many as possible including our Jed. So we bit our tongues and gave him a mail asking if he could list both the Agia Napa studios and the Fuller off-plans. We gave him our asking prices and awaited a call back from him. He was just going to be the first of many agents that we'd get these studios listed with. Just another link in the chain.

The next day just as Dawn had advised us, we took a trip over to Paphos to get our apartments listed with as many of the Paphos Estate Agents as we could. We stopped off at the project site first of all to see for ourselves exactly what stage the building works were at. The donkey had long since been evicted and now all the walls were erected. It was still the bare bones of the build, but apparently once the walls are built and the roof is on they consider this 75% built. It was far from finished, but progress was definitely being made. Maybe they would have this project finished by September after all, but quite honestly we had no wish to be around to see it. We needed to sell, because judging by the stage they were at on the build, we would be getting asked for that next 60% pretty soon.

We had seen enough. Now it was time to get these studios sold. Let the games begin!!! The first big estate agency was on the route back, so we decided to pull in there first to see what they could do for us. The agency was Purchase Cyprus one of the biggest on the island. We were curious, not sure what to expect, after all we weren't asking them to list something that was completed. These were still very much off-plans. Plans in hand we entered into their office but it soon became very clear that this was not going to be as easy as we had hoped.

Our hopes soon began to melt away under the heat of the woman's frown, as she stared sympathetically at the Fuller plans that we were grasping on to for dear life. We stood in front of her and began to reel off our story, but it was clear that she had already heard it before. In mid flow she interrupted us, "These are Fuller projects then I take it?" she enquired as she nodded at the plans that we held.

"Yes that's right," we answered knowing by the look on her face that something was up.

"Oh!" she paused and nodded her head slowly, clearly trying to find the right words to say next. Like a doctor having to tell the family some bad news, she continued. "I'm sorry but we won't list any Fuller projects. It's our company policy. There are just too many problems with them."

We got the distinct impression that we weren't the first to pop into this office clenching Fuller off plans for sale, and we guessed we wouldn't be the last. We thought we were being clever, but clearly others had had the same idea as us. Mind you, our Fuller project was No 22, so you could imagine there were twenty-one projects in front of us, with twenty-one lots of people all at some point coming to the same realisation as us. Then, like us, having the bright idea to get them listed with other agencies. Probably, like us, going to see their projects progress first of all, then getting down to business from there and the first agency on route back to Paphos main town being Purchase Cyprus.

We clearly weren't the first as the woman explained, "Yes, sorry. We are always getting Fuller people coming in here wanting us to list their properties, but we just can't. The manager's out at the moment but if you want to call him tomorrow I'm sure he'll be glad to explain things in more detail."

No explanation was needed. It was becoming pretty clear that we were stuffed. We exited and carried on with the mission. I mean, Purchase Cyprus were only one agency and there were after all, loads of them. But the story was always the same. None

of them would touch these off-plans with so much as a barge
pole and all of them had heard of Fuller and were not impressed
at all. Horror stories began to emerge of the poor build quality
of these projects. Also, the common consensuses from all these
agencies was that Fuller were building these apartment blocks in
areas where the demand is for villas. Not good for a reselling
point of view.

One of the agents was particularly informative. She told as
how Fuller had a terrible reputation and many, like ourselves,
were being stuck with sub-standard apartments, unable to sell
them. So much for only using quality developers for all their
projects! She told us that they represented any developer who
walked in the door and asked them too. The worst thing that
she told us was that in Cyprus any Tom, Dick or Harry can call
themselves a "developer" and what's been happening, is that
these people are finding themselves with land, and in order to
get the best price from it they call themselves "developers,"
get a company set up and get Fuller to market them to unsuspecting mugs like us and build them. Of course the build quality is terrible.

Fuller doesn't care because they are making their five
percent. She thought the whole thing stank! We wished that we
had smelt the stench before we had signed up for them! To
hammer home her point she told us how in Paphos alone there
are currently over four hundred and fifty so called "developers".
If we still weren't convinced she showed us a property that she
currently had on her books. It was a woman's Fuller property. A
one bedroom apartment. It was completed and they had had it
listed for over a year now. What, a year and no sale you're probably asking, as indeed we were? Well, she told us how the whole
building was absolutely terrible. The workmanship was the
worst she had seen!

People initially took possession of these properties before

any provision for electricity or mains water had been provided, and had waited for months before they were finally supplied, although, Fuller doesn't have the monopoly on doing this. We had heard stories of other big companies letting people move in before these provisions had been made. She told us where this Fuller project was, so we went to take a look for ourselves to see if things were really as bad as she had been making out. We were praying that they weren't but had the terrible feeling that they were!

The first thing we noticed as we pulled up outside the block in question, was the numerous "for sale" signs that were hanging from nearly every apartment. This was definitely not a good sign at all!!! The words on the side of the block read, Fuller Project 2. This must have been one of the first Fuller projects. We took some hope from that at least. Maybe by now, twenty projects later they had got better. The only trouble was that this theory didn't really hold up since they are using lots of different developers. The best you could hope for was that your particular developers were half decent!

Anyway, as we wondered around this development it soon became blindingly clear that the lady was not exaggerating. It was an absolute disgrace and an insult to all the true credible developers out there. Whoever the developers were on this one, they clearly only had one thing on their minds, and it wasn't pride in their work that's for sure! My guess, judging by the substandard, cheap materials they had used was that the only thing they were thinking of was money. Namely profit. The doors to each block were of the worst quality. With a gaping gap of about three inches beneath them and gaps around the frame from where no one had bothered to seal them, I would have to say that they stood about as much chance of stopping any rain or wind coming in as a bamboo hut!

As we entered and walked up the stairs facing us was a

window, which due to the warped frame it was precariously perched in, could not shut. First landing, whoever put the light sockets in and door bells must have been pissed. Either that or the building had shifted 45 degrees since they had been installed. With this building, that was a distinct possibility! As we continued upwards we came across, for me, the most horrifying part of this building. We came up to the top of the stairwell and straight out onto the flat roof, three stories up. Note that I did not mention having to open any door. This is not just a lazy mistake on my part. No, there was no door whatsoever.

Probably too much expense for any developer to bother installing a door to the mere roof. I mean, what's the point in it after all? Well apart from the obvious, stopping the wind and rain from coming inside, not that any of their doors had much chance of doing that. There were also the safety implications. Let's just say that I wouldn't want my kids any where near this building. As you walk out onto the roof, there are no walls or railings to stop anyone from falling straight over the edge. Pipes and cables are laden all over it like spaghetti, making it easy to trip and fall at any time. A door, preferably with a lock on it would at least prevent any adventurous children from venturing up onto this death trap!

We quickly made our way off the roof and back down to relative safety. Although relative is the key word here. Around the poor excuse for a swimming pool were exposed rusty metal spikes sticking up out of the concrete ready to pierce some poor soul's foot. Walking around the building, much of the external rendering had fallen from the walls and was left in shattered pieces on the floor below. The building looked as if it were twenty years old, not the one year that it was. The cherry on top of the cake, so to speak, was the old plastic bucket that sat smack bang in the middle of the driveway. It was stuck solid in the concrete with the top half of it sticking out, handle and all. Who knows what bizarre purpose this bucket served but there it was nevertheless!

I have to say in our particular Fuller projects defence that this one, unlike ours, appeared to have no redeeming features. It was in a terrible location with no sea views or even any sort of decent views at all. The design of the actual development was awful. At least ours was a far nicer design and would have some lovely views when it was finally finished. Ours was situated in a much better location but it was still a Fuller project nevertheless, and if we were to expect the same quality workmanship that was clearly on display here on ours, then we were in deep shit!!!

If before we were unsure of the bad decision that we had made to purchase our Fuller off-plans, now we were in no doubt. Anger swept over us at our stupidity to let someone like Jed talk us into buying these stupid studios. We hadn't fallen for time shares when they were offered to us or pyramid selling, Amway and alike, so how on earth had we let ourselves fall for this Fuller con? And make no mistake, a con it is and a good con at that.

Just to make it very clear let me explain how this con works. It all works on the basic fact that it's far easier to get people to part with less money than more. Getting people to believe that they will never have to pay the full amount for something, i.e. these apartments, encourages them to buy more since they've only got to put down a relatively small amount. Like us, instead of only buying one you sign up for two or more. Thus more are sold and Fuller make more sales commission. All because these mugs believe that they will never have to pay the full amount.

Just remember that despite all the promises of reselling before the full price is required, you have signed a legal document that in fact says that you have agreed to purchase these properties. You have not signed anything that ties Fuller to their hollow promises of selling them on. Ultimately, you are the ones who have the burden of selling on, something that as you can see, quite frankly cannot be sold on until it is completed and fully paid for. It is as I say, a great scam! You have to admire it for that at least.

Also, to make it even better, most people won't tell anyone one about it for fear of not being able to sell their apartments on once this scam is out in the open. After all, once it is, no one in their right mind would touch anything, off-plan or finished, from companies like Fuller. Would they? Before you sign up for anything like this you must do your homework. You must check the developer's previous work. If you can't find any previous work from them, then do not sign. Do as we did, but do it right at the start before you sign anything. Go around to all of the local Estate Agents and ask what they think about whoever you're about to do a deal with. Do not get lazy. This relative small amount of time could save you a lot of future stress and money, so believe me, it's well worth it. Why oh why had we not read a book like this one before we signed up for the Fuller shite???

As fate would have it, soon after leaving Fuller's project number two, we had a phone call from none other that our Jed! It was at this point extremely difficult to refrain from showing this man the contempt that we felt for him. He was calling in response to the mail we had sent him regarding listing all our stuff. He told us that he could do it. Of course he could, I mean it was no skin off his nose was it? He asked us if we were sure about the price we were listing them at, because we had to take into consideration his five percent to come off- as if we didn't know! We explained that we were making absolutely no money on these and that in fact we'd be loosing money on them, could he not lower his commission?

You would have expected some sort of guilt from him, I mean after all, he was the one who sold us this shite in the first place. But no sympathy or apologies were offered instead out right cheek. The audacity of the man was beyond belief! In reply, he started to tell us how after two percent going to his contacts in England, he would only be left with three percent for himself, so anything less than five percent from us wouldn't be worth his while. Oh excuse us while we wipe away our tears. What a damned cheek. At three percent he'd make approximately £1035 CYP per apartment, not bad for doing nothing. Considering he had also made commission on the initial sale of this crap to us. Even if he only took one percent he'd still make £690 CYP for the two off plans, and the same again for the Agia Napa studios- we'll be losing more than that!

But there was absolutely no sympathy or leeway given. Instead, he expected us to be sympathetic of *his* plight! What a complete creep! But as I've said before, this creep was all we had, and agents, like Jed, are unfortunately a necessary evil! So, reluctantly we agreed. I'm pretty sure Jed knew we were pissed by the tone of our voices. He had started off as a lovable school teacher type and had slowly transformed into the weasel he really is. Between you and me, now all we see when we look at him is a pointed nosed weasel!!!

I have to say looking back to when Jed worked his voodoo on us and sold us these two Fuller beauties, he made it sound so complicated. Quite honestly, it's only now that we've really finally got our heads around the whole concept. Looking back we were complete and utter fools. If you don't fully understand something don't go ahead with it! The only thing that Jed made sound easy was the profit we'd make. Well the truth is there's never such a thing as an easy buck, and if you're foolish enough to fall for that old nugget then you deserve everything that you get! However, we clearly weren't the only ones who had fallen for it, and as far as not understanding the concept of the whole thing, well, even Dawn, their own agent didn't!

But now I do understand it, it's really quite simple. If Jed had explained it in the way I'm about to we would never have bought them. Quite simply, the money you could make would equate to the appreciation of your property, minus the costs i.e. Estate Agents fees & solicitor fees etc. If you sell for less you will obviously lose money. If you sell for the same price, you will lose money. To be completely clear, you will only make any money if you sell for a lot more than your purchase price. Now this is all very well if the property market does keep on rising and your property manages to acquire a good amount of appreciation, but contrary to what the Estate Agents will have you believe, property markets don't always rise. Frankly, if they don't you're stuffed and you can kiss your "potential returns" together with a large proportion, if not all, of your money goodbye!!!

While I'm on the subject of scams, I feel an obligation to warn you of one more. This one's cleverly designed to entrap the would be foreign "buy-to-let investor" with more money than sense. Amazingly enough, this is not one that we fell for ourselves, but have subsequently heard about through very reliable sources (I'll tell you a bit more about our sources later).

'Guaranteed rentals!' That's right, guaranteed. Not just verbal either!!! All above board and in writing! They're guaranteeing set rental returns and management, for seven months a year for two whole years. Can't be bad? Well, this is certain developer's ploy, in a long line of ploys, to encourage more sales of their ever growing fields of "luxury villas." Villas that otherwise would not have a demand for, if not for the good old buy-to-let'ers. Villas built in areas that just do not have the rental demand that the developers are saying exists.

How can you go wrong with a written guarantee I can hear you muttering? Well, let me enlighten you. The scam goes something like this… Quite simply, the properties they are selling are over priced. When you come to Cyprus to view, probably on one of their free tickets, they'll escort you around for your whole stay. They'll pretty much eat and sleep with you, and even kindly take you to some of the sites if you're lucky. Well, you can be sure as hell they are not just doing this because they are such "nice" people. They are doing this to limit the amount of time you have by yourself. Time that you could discover the fact that you could buy similar properties for a third less.

As a result of this overpricing, they have cleverly worked out that they can very well afford to take the loss of the supposed rental for the seven months a year for two years that they will pay you. Yes, that's right, they will indeed pay you this money as agreed out of their own pockets. They will, as agreed, pay you even if you're property is not rented out, and surprisingly enough, most of them aren't. Loads of them are as we speak sitting there hauntingly vacant. The problem is as follows. The people buying these are once again, buying them specifically to rent out, but after two years the developers are washing their hands of them, as per the contracts. The money stops and suddenly the reality kicks in. They are finding themselves with un-rentable properties. Once again, worst of all, due to the ever increasing amounts of these properties coming on the market, they are also finding out that selling ain't gonna be no walk in the park either. Shit!!!

Be very wary of this one. Try to do your homework to see whether the demand for rentals at the price you need is really a reality. Do not just take what the good old Estate Agent tells you as gospel. Talk to the locals. You know, the guy behind the bar, or in our case the local property maintenance company. You might just discover a completely different story being told!!! One more problem to watch for with the above deal, other than the fact that you will be unable to stay in your own new "luxury" villa during the summer, is that people are finding themselves in trouble when it comes to the winter months. This is the period that most of these developers are not covering for "rentals" or more importantly maintenance. However, it is in these months that most damage can occur. The pools still need treating and who knows what the storms will do. Tiles off, flooding etc. etc. etc. Who will be keeping an eye on your property and how much will it all cost??? Think deeper!!!

CHAPTER 22

Here And Now

I suppose the real question you're dying to know is, how did it all work out for us? Well we've been out here now for just over a year and despite everything, have no desire to return back to the U.K. I suppose that says it all really.

We still haven't sold our Fuller off-plans, and are now paying the interest until the build is complete, with the hope of being able to sell them at that point. At least we'll be able to get them listed with other agents anyway. Thanks to the likes of Jed and Fuller, we had purchased two properties that we had absolutely no desire to own.

Our two studios in Agia Napa sold relatively easily to another young couple much like ourselves buying them as a buy-to-let investment. One half of us wanted to tell this couple not to buy them, but the other half told us to think of ourselves and unfortunately, the hard truth is that this is a dog eat dog world as we found out ourselves. All we can say to them is, we wish them all the best of luck, they'll need it. Needless to say, after all the fees and the repayment of the mortgage that we had on them were deducted we did make our predicted loss.

It could have been far worse, but at least now most of our original investment money was safely back in our bank account earning us interest and ready for us to put to use in our next projects. This we did, and by doing so earned far more than any off-plan pie in the sky crap, or buy-to-let nightmare. Currently, we are on our forth project. We successfully renovated and sold our Kilani property in May, nearly a year after our arrival. Funnily enough, we sold to the very same Czech who brought Titanic. As luck would have it, he was completely happy with the apartment and wanted a mountain property for his gran to reside in. Somewhere he and his family could also escape the scorching heat of mid-summer. It was fantastic news for us, as it meant a quick sale and no Estate Agents fees. Result! We made a grand profit of £60k CYP on that one so that was fantastic ☺.

Not such good news on our two bed in Germasogeia. We never did see the works through to the end, but we did at least get the ball rolling. Unfortunately, it was proving to be way too difficult to get everyone together to pay their money. Whilst we did manage to collect most of the maintenance money in, there were still one or two who blatantly refused to cooperate. To get the much needed works done, we really were going to have to take these people to court, which apart from the time and money involved, was going to be yet more stress for us and we had had just about all the stress we ever wanted to take.

So when an opportunity to purchase a detached house with loads of land came up, we grabbed it with both hands. It meant selling our flat before the works were completed at a far reduced rate than we otherwise would have achieved. We still completely renovated it inside to a really high standard however, and got our desired quick sale for it in March. The couple who brought it were really happy with it. To be honest, they got a really good deal on it because it was in a fantastic location, and once the works were completed, this building was going to be worth far more (now I'm starting to sound like an Estate Agent! ☺).

Demis (the flat's committee President) was now quite capable and determined to carry on with pushing the works through.

Most of the people there were willing to pay for the works, and I was very confident that in this case, it would really materialise. It was just going to take a bit longer than we had first hoped for. I felt a bit bad leaving Demis to carry on alone, but ultimately we all must think of ourselves at the end of the day, and I'm sure that if Demis had had the opportunity of moving out and into a detached house somewhere, we wouldn't have seen him for the dust. Demis was the only one there that I did have any sympathy for, simply because the rest of them had been sitting on their arses for years, allowing this building to get into such a state and should have done something themselves to sort it out years ago!

Anyway, we made a total profit of £15k CYP on that one. Not the best, but considering the problems with the building, we were pretty happy with it. The money from it we put towards our house project that we had just purchased. This was to be our fourth real renovation project. We would transform this run down two bedroom house into a beautiful four bedroom house. By building another floor on top, we'll be getting the most magnificent sea views right across Limassol, something they didn't realise when they sold it to us!

So just over a year in and we've successfully renovated and sold 3 projects and managed to offload our 2 Agia Napa studios. While we work on transforming the house, we are currently negotiating our next project. Our own house. A beautiful detached country house up in Troodos with views to kill for, at least it will be when we've finished with it! All we had dreamed of, and a far cry from our old lives in the smog of London. No, at this stage we definitely do not have any desire to return.

Our first year in Cyprus was truly an experience in which we received our diplomas from the school of hard knocks. It was a gruelling crash course that I would not wish to put anyone through. However, you know what they say, sometimes the only way to learn is from your mistakes and god knows we made our fair share! As I've said before, I hope after reading this you won't make the same mistakes as us, but if the above saying is true then you probably will! If so, my advice to you is to buy some hair dye because you'll probably need it to dye the grey hairs that you'll inevitably going to acquire ☺.

As much as I have cursed the Estate Agents, they are unfortunately a necessary evil, unless you are as we were with our Kilani project, fortunate enough to be able to get a buyer without going through them. One thing is for sure, we only managed to dig ourselves out of the mountain of crap we had got ourselves into by being out here. I think if we weren't, we would not have stood a chance in hell. This is something to seriously consider if you are still thinking of investing in a foreign country.

In our experience, buy-to-lets were definitely not for us, and once again, if you are considering them and are planning to manage them from another country, I would seriously think again. It was hard enough managing them from here, but I fear almost impossible from another country.

We learnt that if you are buying resale apartments, really make sure that the building is good and that the residents are good, and all pay towards the maintenance of it. Don't be blinded by great sea views! Consider the bigger picture. Only use builders, lawyers etc. whom you can communicate with. Communication is the most important thing in any business, and something that not too many locals here seem too good at. Try, if possible, to get recommendations. Only now, have we really got a great team of people together, but a great team is essential to make things work.

If you are going to venture into any off-plan money making schemes, make sure you fully understand exactly what it is that you are venturing into. If after understanding fully, you *do* venture into it be sure to remember that you can loose as well as win, and despite what agents may claim there are never any guarantees. If you do loose in such schemes then you've only got yourselves to blame. After all, the Jed's of this world are only doing their jobs... They worship but one god, and his name is COMMISION!!!

The End so Far!!!

P.S. There's just one last thing that I feel I should add to this whole story of ours. This really is a case of fact being stranger than fiction, although by this time we were getting quite used to it. As fate would have it, just after I had finished my draft version of this story, we had an unexpected phone call in from one of the Estate Agents that we had dealt with. I'll name no names, but rest assured, it was not Fuller!

The irony of their offer was too irresistible for us to refuse, bearing in mind all of the above that I have just spent the past 1 year writing about. They wanted *us* of all people, to be the faces of their major add campaign to promote their company. They had just purchased 60 minutes of airtime on Sky and wanted us to give a 2 minute endorsement, promoting all the good things about our time in Cyprus, Cyprus in general, and of course, themselves, The Estate Agents!!! ☺.

Disclaimer

As I stated at the beginning of the story, this is only based on our personal experiences. We also changed the names of every person and company we came across, so if any of the names happen to be the same as anyone or company you know, this is purely coincidental and the comments were not written about them. If you do feel that you sound like any of the characters in the book….then maybe you have a guilty conscience??

Printed in the United Kingdom
by Lightning Source UK Ltd.
124592UK00001B/119/A